GLIMPSE
AN IRISH FELON'S
PRISON LIFE

By

THOMAS J. CLARKE

First published in 1922

Read &' Co.

Copyright © 2020 Read & Co. History

This edition is published by Read & Co. History,
an imprint of Read & Co.

British Library Cataloguing-in-Publication Data
A catalogue record for this book is available
from the British Library.

Read & Co. is part of Read Books Ltd.
For more information visit
www.readandcobooks.co.uk

CONTENTS

THE
PROVISIONAL
GOVERNMENT OF THE
IRISH REPUBLIC

TO THE PEOPLE OF IRELAND

IRISHMEN AND IRISHWOMEN:

In the name of God and of the dead generations from which she receives her old tradition of nationhood, Ireland, through us, summons her children to her flag and strikes for her freedom.

Having organised and trained her manhood through her secret revolutionary organisation, the Irish Republican Brotherhood, and through her open military organisations, the Irish Volunteers and the Irish Citizen Army, having patiently perfected her discipline, having resolutely waited for the right moment to reveal itself, she now seizes that moment, and supported by her exiled children in America and by gallant allies in Europe, but relying in the first on her own strength, she strikes in full confidence of victory.

We declare the right of the people of Ireland to the ownership of Ireland and to the unfettered control of Irish destinies, to be sovereign and indefeasible. The long usurpation of that right by a foreign people and government has not extinguished the right, nor can it ever be extinguished except by the destruction of the Irish people. In every generation the Irish people have asserted their right to national freedom and sovereignty; six times during the past three hundred years they have asserted it in arms. Standing on that fundamental right and again asserting it in arms in the face of the world, we hereby proclaim the Irish Republic as a Sovereign Independent State, and we pledge our lives and the lives of our comrades in arms to the cause of its freedom, of its welfare, and of its exaltation among the nations. The Irish Republic is entitled to, and hereby claims, the allegiance of every Irishman and Irishwoman. The Republic guarantees religious and civil liberty, equal rights and equal opportunities to all its citizens, and declares its resolve to pursue the happiness and prosperity of the whole nation and of all its parts, cherishing all the children of the nation equally, and oblivious of the differences carefully fostered by an alien Government, which have divided a minority from the majority in the past.

Until our arms have brought the opportune moment for the establishment of a permanent National Government, representative of the whole people of Ireland and elected by the suffrages of all her men and women, the Provisional Government, hereby constituted, will administer the civil and military affairs of the Republic in trust for the people.

We place the cause of the Irish Republic under the protection of the Most High God, Whose blessing we invoke upon our arms, and we pray that no one who serves that cause will dishonour it by cowardice, inhumanity, or rapine. In this supreme hour the Irish nation must, by its valour and discipline, and by the readiness of its children to sacrifice themselves for the common good, prove itself worthy of the august destiny to which it is called.

Signed on behalf of the Provisional Government,,

THOMAS J. CLARKE, SEAN MAC DIARMADA,
P. H. PEARSE, JAMES CONNOLLY, THOMAS MACDONAGH,
EAMONN CEANNT, JOSEPH PLUNKETT

INTRODUCTION

" But it seemed safe to classify as dangerous those who were credibly reported to be in more than occasional or chance communication with some one or more of the small group of persons known in Dublin to be dangerously seditious, e.g., T. J. Clarke."—Evidence of Mr. A. H. Norway at the Hardinge Commission.

THOMAS J. CLARKE was born in Hurst Castle, Isle of Wight, on the 11th March, 1857, of Irish parents, his father, who was a soldier, being from Galway and his mother from Tipperary. Shortly after Tom's birth the family went to South Africa, and when he was about ten years old returned and settled down in Dungannon, of which town he always regarded himself as a native. He left Ireland for America in 1881, and returned in 1883 on a special mission from the Clanna-Gael, as a result of which he was arrested and, in May 1883, sentenced to penal servitude for life, serving actually $15\frac{1}{2}$ years, and being released in September 1898. He went to America again in 1899, and returned in 1907 and settled in Dublin, where he went into business as tobacconist and newsagent. He was the first Signatory to the Proclamation of the Irish Republic, and was shot in Kilmainham Jail on the 3rd May, 1916, aged 59 years.

I first met Tom Clarke in, I think, 1909, and in the years of close association that followed came to know him well and to love him well. To all the young men of the Separatist movement of that time he was a help and an inspiration. And he was surely the exception in his own generation, the one shining example. It was a time of struggle in the Separatist movement, a time when the least little thing might have tilted the balance the wrong way, when, as it happened, Tom Clarke tilted it the right way. There comes in every movement a time when there is a clash between the younger generation and the older generation, and that clash was brewing in the I. R. B. just about that time. There was, on the one hand, the older generation which had got into a groove, which had no policy for the movement save the policy of keeping the spirit alive, which in effect throttled all attempt at a forward policy and believed that nothing in the way of action was possible. And there was, on the other hand, the younger generation, which believed in a forward movement, wanted a forward movement, and believed in its own capacity to run such a movement. After a long period of splits, a period during which the young men as a whole had avoided it, the I. R. B. had at last succeeded in closing up its ranks, and in those ranks were plenty of the young men, men with vision and purpose, men who wanted to do something. And naturally and inevitably they pushed to the front. They were regarded by the older men with some alarm, as people who by some rashness, by some disregard of the policy of giving no signs of life, would imperil the whole movement. And it was inevitable that there should be a struggle. For a good while it was a silent, an almost imperceptible struggle, but it came to a head in the autumn of 1912, and the young men won, won only just in time. Tom Clarke had stood with us from the first, and I can still remember the thrill of pleased surprise with which I saw him, after I first met him, stand for every proposal which the other men of his generation frowned at and would down. One thing in particular which all of us had at heart, and a thing which eventually had a profound influence in the right direction on the whole development of thought in Ireland, the starting of *Irish Freedom*, was due wholly to Tom. We young men had a paper as our first thought, but before we thought the time opportune to propose it the proposal came from Tom Clarke, and we carried it. The result was *Irish Freedom*, which gave to the Separatist movement in Ireland unity and philosophy, and which had an influence in making the Ireland of to-day which has not yet been recognised. We all worked for it without stint and without cessation, and Tom Clarke as keenly and as effectively as the youngest amongst us.

The full story of the Insurrection of 1916 will some day be given publicity : but apart from the actual details of the events leading up to it, it is time that the main event, the really proximate cause of it, should be stated clearly and unequivocably. And that was that the I. R. B., working since 1911 under a Supreme Council who were united and who knew where they were going, had prepared for an insurrection, had prepared the mind of the organisation, and through that a great deal of Ireland, so as to make it fit to seize the opportunity when it did come. And when everybody else in Ireland had gone rotten in 1914, the I. R. B., and as much of the Irish Volunteers as it influenced, stood fast by its principles and prepared, a handful against an Empire, for insurrection. The first meeting of the Supreme Council of the I. R. B. which was held after the outbreak of war between England and Germany, a meeting held in the middle of August 1914, decided to organise an insurrection in Ireland before the war ended. And it did it. It stuck to its policy and its purpose firmly, and the insurrection of Easter Week was the result. It was neither a *Sinn Féin* Insurrection nor a Socialist-Labour insurrection, as it has been variously labelled, but a Fenian Insurrection, in direct descent from Stephens, Mitchel, and Wolfe Tone.

In that policy and decision, Tom Clarke was foremost. He stood to all of us as a strength and an inspiration, and emphatically as a comrade. His life and his unconquerable will and his work and his energy made him easily the first of us and the best of us. And amid all the jokes and easiness that marked our intercourse, we all knew that we were in the presence of one who stood as the embodiment of Fenianism, an impregnable rock. More than any other one man he was responsible for the insurrection, for he was the mainstay of the group which from 1911 had worked and planned for an insurrection, whose faith and position were so finely set out in 1916 by Padraig Pearse in his four undying pamphlets.

All that has been forgotten by the younger generation, if it ever knew it, but it was not forgotten by those who worked with Tom. And their recognition of that, their unanimous and public recognition, was the calling upon him to be the first to sign the proclamation of 1916. When everything was ready for signature the other men insisted that he should have the honour of signing first. He demurred at first, saying that he did not think that he was worthy of that honour, but they insisted, they said that he had been their inspiration and their pilot, and that none of them would sign except after him, and then he signed. He was, I think, genuinely surprised and touched to find that his comrades thought so highly of himself and his work, for he himself was modest and retiring by nature, and never by any chance thought of himself. But the honour they did him was his, clearly and unmistakably, by right of his life and his work and his example.

This book will, perhaps, be appreciated most by those who knew Tom. His personality is all through it like a framework, and the writing, terse, crisp, and always to the point, is exactly as he used to speak. One cannot read it without being reminded at every turn of the lean figure with worn frame but unconquerable soul that used to stand for hours behind a shop counter, selling papers and tobacco to all and sundry and exchanging jokes with his more intimate friends. A man who has been through fifteen years of prison ought, I suppose, to be broken-spirited and inert ; but Tom Clarke was as supple as steel and as spontaneous in laughter as a boy. The casual visitor would never imagine that he had been fifteen years in prison.

But, in addition to its immediate interest as an intimate revelation of the personality of the first signatory to the Republican Proclamation, it will have a permanent place also in prison literature. Literature is perhaps the last word which he himself would have thought of applying to it : he never looked upon himself as an intellectual, and would have characterised the articles as a mere jotting down of interesting facts. But they are more than that. Those who come to the book expecting a recital of prison cruelties will be disappointed as will those who expect bitterness, querulousness, thirst for revenge, or any other of the less admirable qualities which imprisonment of the drastic nature portrayed is apt to induce. It would be futile to suppose that fifteen years of such a life as his prison life did not affect him, or that it left him amicably disposed towards those responsible for it. But he always regarded himself as a soldier of the Irish Republic, to whom prison and suffering were the day's work : he nerved himself against prison and bore it, largely because of his proud consciousness of the cause he stood for : it was his proudest glory that " one of the Irish rank and file " could neither be bent nor broken by deliberately cruel treatment ; and he came out of prison, shaken indeed, steeled and hardened in the sense that he had developed an intense energy for national work and a contempt for drones, but clear-headed, vital, and neither warped nor embittered. In the ordinary way he never referred to his prison life at all, he was too busy doing national work of one kind or another to waste any time brooding over the past, or fulminating empty abuse against those responsible. And in the same spirit he wrote these chapters, recounting his prison experiences almost wholly from the personal and human aspect, with a lack of passion and an absence of rhetoric unusual considering what he had gone through. I do not know that Irish prison literature contains any better writing of its kind than the bulk of these chapters.

His political principles were always clear. He stood for the full national demand—for separation—and he would neither work for, nor accept anything less than that. Other movements —the Gaelic League, the Industrial Revivals, the old *Sinn Féin* movement, had his sympathy, but he regarded them all as subsidiary to the main political ideal of separation, holding that the only Ireland which would ever be worth anything in the world would be an Ireland absolutely her own mistress. That ideal he held, not alone as an ultimate ideal, but also as an immediate ideal, and he never adopted the course which so many Separatists adopted of supporting actively the old *Sinn Féin* Policy as a practical and workable policy pending developments. " *Sinn Féin*," he used to say, " is all right as far as it goes, but it doesn't go far enough." And he never lost that faith, which every Separatist has, that some time or other the mass of the people would, as he used to put it, " line up " on the right side.

If I say a last word on his reasonableness, it is because so many people have assumed that his uncompromising political views were the result of his imprisonment. But, like Rossa, he was " an Irishman since he was born," and his imprisonment, while it certainly strengthened his political faith, left him without bitterness and utterly without that passion for revenge which is ascribed to him. He worked and planned against England all his days, but it was not so much against England as for Ireland. Those who are so fond of accusing Separatists of mere hatred probably never met one outside the pages of the *Irish Times*, and certainly never gave five minutes consecutive thought to the historical justification of the Separatist principle. It is an absolute impossibility for any Irishman who knows anything considerable of Irish history to have any real faith in any settlement short of Separation. In every generation in Ireland there have been men and women of that faith, who can be induced by no plausibility yet invented to forego one jot of the full claim of Ireland, whose opposition to English rule in Ireland is an opposition, not to bad government of the country, but to foreign government of the country, and who would take up arms just as cheerfully and remorselessly against an Imperialised Irish Government as against any purely English Government : believing that no settlement which does not give Ireland complete and absolute freedom, internal and external, and full power to organise her resources to defend that freedom, is worth more than the paper it is written on.

It was the happiness of Tom Clarke to have linked up in his person two such uncompromising groups, to have been on the one hand a young man in the fighting forces of Fenianism after '67, and on the other hand a (comparatively) old man in the fighting forces of 1916. As a man who had spent fifteen of his best years in prison for Ireland, nobody could have cavilled at him had he left the work to younger men, but in heart and in mind he was as young as the youngest, and no man of them made the supreme sacrifice more proudly or whole-heartedly. He had the great gift of a great faith in his country, and he held firmly to the principles that are now proclaimed by the majority of Nationalists at a time when they seemed for ever snowed under. It has been recorded by one of the survivors that he addressed the men before the surrender at the G. P. O., and reconciled them to the surrender by giving it as his opinion that the fight which had been made had saved Ireland, and that he, after his life's work, was satisfied. And he has been proved right. Ireland to-day places him and his comrades in that Valhalla where sit Tone, Emmet, and Fitzgerald ; they have an indelible place in the memory of the Nation.

P. S. O'HEGARTY

GLIMPSES OF AN
IRISH FELON'S PRISON LIFE

I

EARLY PRISON THOUGHTS

I AM not going to attempt to give anything like a complete history of my prison life. In the short space at my disposal that is out of the question. A detailed and connected history of nearly sixteen years' experience in English dungeons cannot possibly be crushed into so short a narrative. Such a history would in addition be largely uninteresting, and would mean the repetition of much that has been recounted by my fellow-prisoners, John Daly and James F. Egan.

Prison life had for me really two sides—the dismal, dark side, full of wretchedness and misery, that even now I cannot think of without shuddering, and, strange as it may seem, the bright side too, the side which I can now look back upon with some degree of pleasure and pride. 'Tis true there was not much of this, while of the other there was an unconscionable quantity. Looking back now, and comparing the dark with the bright side, I get a picture, as it were, of a few glimmering stars—bright spots here and there in a black, thunder-laden sky—and as it is likely to be more interesting, I will try to bring the bright side into prominence, and keep the dark side as much as possible in the background. The dark side of prison life for an Irish prisoner in an English convict prison is so hideously wretched that, in any case, I should despair of ever being able to describe it adequately. Had anyone told me before the prison doors closed upon me that it was possible for any human being to endure what the Irish prisoners have endured in Chatham Prison, and come out of it alive and sane, I would not have believed him, yet some have done so, and it has been a source of perpetual surprise to me that I was able to get through it at all.

We must go back to April 1883 at the Old Bailey, London. Dr. Gallagher, Alfred Whitehead, John Curtin, and myself had been convicted of treason-felony, after a week's trial, before Lord Chief Justice Coleridge and two other judges. Immediately the Lord Chief Justice passed the sentence (penal servitude for life) we were hustled out of the dock into the prison van, surrounded by a troop of mounted police, and driven away at a furious pace through the howling mobs that thronged the streets from the Courthouse to Millbank Prison. London was panic-stricken at the time, and the hooting and yelling with which the street mobs used to assail us, going to and from the Courthouse whilst the trial lasted, need not be further noticed. A few hours later saw us in prison dress, with close-cropped heads —" Penal Servitude for Life " had begun. That same day the rules and regulations were read to us. Nothing in them startled me like the one that stated, " Strict silence must at all times be observed ; under no circumstances must one prisoner speak to another." When I thought of what that meant in conjunction with another paragraph, " No hope of release for life prisoners till they have completed twenty years, and then each case will be decided on its own merits," and remembered with what relentless savagery the English Government has always dealt with the Irishmen it gets into its clutches, the future appeared as black and appalling as imagination could picture it. But the worst my imagination could then picture of English brutality was outdone by the horrors of Chatham Prison that I was afterwards to experience.

In Millbank the surveillance was so close and continuous that we found it impossible to speak to each other. I tried twice, but was dropped on on both occasions. However, we were able to communicate with each other in spite of all their watchfulness and strictness. We were determined at all costs to be able to send messages. Pen or pencil we had none. What of that! A fellow has no business in prison unless he is resourceful and observant. The gates of our cells turned upon pivots, and the lower of these pivots was embedded in lead. Some one of us noticed this, and, when the officers' back was turned, stole over and managed to dig a bit of the lead out with a point of the scissors (we were employed in tailoring at this time). Presently a note was written on a piece of the regulation brown paper with the lead, giving instructions as to how correspondence could be carried on. Next day that note was shot into the neighbouring cell, under the very nose of the officer, shot in as you would shoot a marble, without any movement of arm or body.

Henceforward while in Millbank we were able to communicate with each other. Of course, we were always liable to be searched when leaving the cell, and when returning to it searched again.

Once or twice in Millbank it so happened that I had a note on special search days, but I contrived to get it out of my clothing and into my mouth unnoticed by the officer at my side. The other prisoners there had, I believe, occasionally to do the same thing, but none of us were ever caught with notes, nor were we ever suspected of carrying on this clandestine correspondence.

Looking back now to my imprisonment in Millbank, I get a picture of a dreary time of solitary confinement in the cold, white-washed cell, with a short daily exercise varying the monotony. Day after day all alike, no change, maddening silence, sitting hopeless, friendless, and alone, with nothing in this world to look forward to but that occasional note coming from some one or other of my comrades, Gallagher, Whitehead, and Curtin, who were in the same plight as myself.

Towards the close of the year 1883 I was roused up very early out of bed one morning and told to dress quickly and come out of my cell. Presently I found myself with Gallagher, Whitehead, and Curtin out in the corridor, and all four of us handcuffed to a gang chain. A strong posse of armed officers surrounded us, and away we were taken to the railway station, and, thus escorted, conveyed to Chatham Prison. Featherstone, Dalton, Deasey, and Flanagan arrived in Chatham about the same time, and another batch of Irish prisoners from Glasgow at the beginning of 1884. A few months later two other Irish prisoners came. I saw them first in Chapel one morning, and, to my grief and surprise, recognised John Daly, whose acquaintance I had made some years before in the North of Ireland, and had again met in America shortly before I left there. His companion, K.561, was James F. Egan, then a stranger to me. We soon came to know each other better, and before long were fast

5

friends, and more loyal or kinder friends, or more manly, self-reliant men I could not wish to have by my side in a fight with the English foe inside those walls, or outside them either. I want no man's opinion of either Daly or Egan. The ordeal they went through under my eyes for years is a test of manhood as severe and searching as mortal man could be subject to, and I know in what spirit they met it and went through it. We three were so closely identified with each other in prison that to speak of my prison life without mentioning them would be impossible.

We treason-felony prisoners were known in Chatham as "The Special Men," and some twelve or fourteen of us were kept, not in the ordinary prison halls, but in the penal cells—kept there so that we could be the more conveniently persecuted, for the authorities aimed at making life unbearable for us. The ordinary rules regulating the treatment of prisoners, which, to some extent, shield them from foul play and the caprice of petty officers, these rules, as far as they did that, were, in our case, set aside, in order to give place to a system devised by the governor of the prison, Captain Harris. This was a scientific system of perpetual and persistent harassing, which gave the officers in charge of us a free hand to persecute us just as they pleased. It was made part of their duty to worry and harass us all the time. Harassing morning, noon, and night, and on through the night, harassing always and at all times, harassing with bread and water punishments, and other punishments, with " no sleep " torture and other tortures. This system was applied to the Irish prisoners, and to them only, and was specially devised to destroy us mentally and physically—to kill or drive insane. It was worked to its utmost against us for six or seven years, and it was during that time that all the men who succumbed went mad. One feature of this system was the " no sleep " torture, and for about four of these years I was kept at the most laborious work in the prison, as moulder in the iron foundry on heavy castings. In addition, I was under special surveillance, and the officers had to pay special attention to me, or, in other words, they must annoy me by every means in their power. At night, jaded in body and mind with the heavy labour of the day and the incessant nagging of the officers, I would return to my cell, and when once inside the door would fling myself on the floor and not move until supper-time. If I went to bed before the bell rang it meant a bread and water punishment, and I was already getting enough of their systematic starvation. When the bell rang I would turn into bed, sometimes to sleep, sometimes to lie awake for hours, with body too weary

7

and nerves too shattered for any refreshing sleep to come. If sleep came I was wakened within an hour by a noise something like the report of a small cannon being fired close beside me. The officer was inspecting us, and had merely banged the heavy iron trap-door after him. With the same loud noise the trap would be banged all through the night at hour intervals. The prisoner might get a few short snatches of sleep between the inspections, or perhaps his nervous system was so shattered with this and other ingenious tortures that he would not be able to sleep at all. This went on night after night, week after week, month after month, for years. Think of the effects of this upon a man's system, and no one will wonder that so many were driven insane by such tactics. The horror of those nights and days will never leave my memory. One by one I saw my fellow-prisoners break down and go mad under the terrible strain—some slowly and by degrees, others suddenly and without warning. "Who next" was the terrible question that haunted us day and night—and the ever-recurring thought that it might be myself added to the agony.

Can I ever forget the night that poor Whitehead realised that he was going mad. There in the stillness, between two of the hourly inspections, I heard the poor fellow fight against insanity, cursing England and

8

English brutality from the bottom of his heart, and beseeching God to strike him dead sooner than allow him to lose his reason. Such episodes are ineffaceable in the memory, they burn their impress into a man's soul.

II

THE INHUMAN TREATMENT OF DR. GALLAGHER

JOHN DALY, James F. Egan, and myself during all those dark and hopeless years had each other's confidence and gave each other support and encouragement. The utmost endeavour of the authorities to crush us failed because we met it in a spirit of defiance, and stood loyally by each other with friendship—aye, with love and sympathy. Every precaution that the prison officers could think of was taken to prevent us "special men" from communicating with each other. The closest surveillance, the utmost vigilance, and savagely severe punishments were awarded us if we were detected. Yet all their vigilance was set at .nought, Daly, Egan, and myself right along were in constant communication with each other. We had our code of signals for communicating to each other by sight—these we owed to Egan ; we had our post office, authorised, not by the Postmaster-General, but by John Daly. Through our post office thousands of notes passed. We had our telephones and our cell telegraph, which latter was introduced by myself very early in our imprisonment.

INHUMAN TREATMENT

A couple of months after Gallagher, Whitehead, Curtin and I arrived in Chatham, sitting in my cell one day racking my brains to find a way to defeat the gaoler's sleepless vigilance the idea of telegraphing suggested itself. All that I could remember about the subject was that the Morse system was based upon two sounds—which were represented on paper by a dot and a dash. The problem was to produce two different kinds of knocks on the wall of the cell and to combine the two sounds into a workable alphabet. After trying different kinds of knocks on my cell table I was satisfied that the dull knock made by the knuckles could not be mistaken for the sharp knock made by a button or slate pencil. I got my slate, and soon had an alphabet worked out. The next question was how to pass the new code to Gallagher The lead with which we had so often written notes I had left behind in Millbank, and there was none to be found in Chatham. Even with lead to write a note it was a matter of great difficulty, so closely were we watched, to pass it on. For months I never spoke to a living soul except to my comrades a few times, and each time it brought me a term of bread and water punishment. However, I was determined to establish the telegraph system. I was working at tailoring at the time, and with a needle and a sheet of brown paper I proceeded to write out the code for Gallagher. Placing the paper on my pillow the letters were formed, perforating the paper with the needle dot by dot—each letter with its corresponding dot and dash. In the same way on other sheets of paper I gave the necessary instructions dot by dot with the point of the needle. It was slow work, especially as the vigilant eye of the officer peeping every now and then into my cell obliged me to conceal the paper when I heard him approaching. It took nearly two days to write that note, but when it was finished it was plain and readable. On the Saturday following I concealed it in my stocking when going out for the weekly bath, and in the bath house managed to get into the next compartment to Gallagher and threw the note over the partition to him. He got it safely, and within a week we were able to converse freely through the wall dividing our cells. On the following Saturday I had another note ready for another of my comrades, and so on week by week till we were able to send telegrams along through six or seven cells.

Being thus closely in touch with Gallagher and Whitehead, as time went on I noticed them change and get queer, and I knew that step by step their reason was giving way. When they were released they were pronounced by the experts who examined them to be hopelessly insane, yet they were no worse then than they had been for the last seven or eight years of their imprisonment.

Everyone inside the prison walls—officers and prisoners—priest, parson, and doctor knew right along that they were insane. The English Home Office knew it, but their vengeance had to be sated whether the victims went mad under the torture or not. For seven or eight years, knowing well that they were insane, the authorities continued to punish them in the most cruel manner for their little irrational acts, for which they were in no sense accountable.

Daly, Egan and myself, although getting it as hard as, and perhaps harder than, our companions, did all we could to have attention drawn to the monstrous inhumanity of their treatment. Governor Harris and his warders simply laughed at us. Many and many a letter that we got to write to our friends outside was filled with denunciations of the way these insane prisoners were treated. Gallagher, Whitehead, Duff, McCabe, Devany, Flanagan, and Casey were all out of their minds at this time. Our letters were, of course, suppressed, and never got farther than the Governor of the prison. I still have a copy of a letter I wrote to Mr. John E. Redmond, who paid me many a visit in prison, and whose kindness on those occasions I can never forget. When this letter was written I managed to make a shorthand copy of it, and this copy, with some other documents, I managed to smuggle out of prison when I was released. The letter was dated June 18th, 1895, but was, of course, suppressed, and never reached its destination. I will quote one part of this letter in order to show the pitiable condition of the insane prisoners and the brutality of the Government in keeping men in such a condition in penal servitude :

" It is nothing directly concerning myself or my case that causes me to take the unusual course of sending you a letter. What I wish to bring under your notice has reference to one of my fellow-prisoners here, J 463, Albert Whitehead. . . . Whitehead is, as you are doubtless aware, one of the unfortunate Irish prisoners whose mind has been shattered by the villainous treatment to which we have been subject. It is now some seven or eight years since he first broke down, and at no time since has he recovered. . . . His fellow-prisoners—or those of them that are not so far gone as himself—are to a man convinced of his insanity, convinced many times over, and you will find all the lately-released Irish prisoners, without a single exception, are of the same opinion. . . . It is true he is not what is called outrageous— the nearest approach to that are the times when he has kept us awake all night long raving at the top of his voice. But although for so far not dangerous to others, he certainly is dangerous to himself, and it is upon this point what I am about to narrate bears.

14

INHUMAN TREATMENT

" One day, a couple of weeks ago, while at work in the carpenter's shop, where he and I are employed, happening to glance round in his direction (the officer was away at the other end of the shop) I saw Whitehead kneeling on the floor gathering something like salt off a board and putting the stuff into his mouth. The stuff was crushed glass. I went over to him, and dropping on my knee beside him caught him by the shoulder and asked him what he was eating glass for. He looked at me with the pitiful, dazed stare that is habitual to him now, and said, ' What, what ! ' I picked up some of the fragments that he had dropped, and again asked him, ' What do you mean by eating this glass ; don't you know it will kill you ? ' He replied in a dull, listless way, ' A pound of it would do you no harm,' and then kept repeating in answer to all my questions, ' A pound of it would do you no harm.' With my handkerchief I dusted away the fragments before him and searched round his bench for more glass. Finding some more I threw it out of the window. All this only occupied a few minutes, and, luckily for me, my ' flagrant violation of the prison rules ' was unobserved by the officer. Had I been seen I would have been visited with a term of bread and water punishment. Just think of it—a whispered word of sympathy to this poor fellow—a single word spoken with a view to prevent him killing himself, and I would receive as severe a punishment as the authorities here inflict on habitual criminals for thieving. And yet here in England they go into hysterics over the horrors and brutality of Siberia and ring the changes on the humanity of the English prison system. ... The truth is that as far as a refined system of cruelty is concerned there is nothing on God's earth to-day to compare with the treatment which we Irish prisoners have been receiving at the hands of the English Government."

I then went on to ask Mr. Redmond to endeavour to have an impartial and competent man sent down to examine into Whitehead's mental state and put a stop to the monstrous cruelty that had been carried on for so many years. As I said before, the letter was suppressed, and is now in the English Home Office, preserved along with my prison record and dozens of other letters I wrote that were likewise never delivered by the authorities.

On the Saturday after I had seen Whitehead swallow the glass I made application to see the prison Catholic chaplain in order to lay the facts before him with a view to try and induce him to move in the matter and try to put a stop to the inhuman treatment of Whitehead. I was taken out of my cell and brought into the chapel, and after a time was ushered into the Sacristy, where I

found Father Matthews sitting on a chair
with his surplice and stole on ready to hear
confessions. I asked him would he allow me
to speak to him outside the confessional, he
consented, and I told him my business concerned Whitehead, who, as he must know,
was quite insane. He said he knew very
well that he was, that as a matter of fact
Whitehead had numbers of times came out
there to him to make his confession, but
knowing he was out of his mind he (Father
Matthews) never gave him absolution, knowing the poor fellow was as incapable of
committing sin as a baby. "Sometimes,"
said he, "Whitehead has come up to the
altar rails on Sunday morning to receive
Holy Communion without even coming out
at all to confession. When he does I
administer the Holy Sacrament to him.
Were I to refuse him, there might be a
scene, and the scandal that would ensue
would, I think, be worse than my giving it
to him." I then told him about Whitehead
swallowing the glass, and asked him to bring
the matter before the authorities. He told
me he couldn't do that. "Why not?" I
inquired. "Were I to tell the Governor this
about Whitehead he would at once ask me
how I knew all that, and I would have to
mention your name, and he would conclude
that you and I had been hobnobbing."
"Well," said I, "what matter—let him."
He replied, "Oh, you don't know the attitude

of those people to me : they would be only too glad to get an opportunity to send me back to my bishop." I must confess I felt very indignant with the priest, and said to him, " Well, if you are afraid to bring this to their attention in order to try and put a stop to such barbarous inhumanity, I am not, and I will do it." He asked, " How ? " I replied, " That's my business," and left him, and was taken back to my cell. Later on the letter to Mr. Redmond was written.

In due course I was notified by the authorities of the suppression of my letter.

I was expecting a visit from Mr. Redmond about this time, and he came to see me soon after. I told him all about the Whitehead affair, and about the letter I had written to himself which had been suppressed. I asked him on his return to London to see the Home Secretary if possible and put the facts before him concerning Whitehead, and suggest to the Home Secretary to have that suppressed letter of mine sent for, and by every means urge him to have an independent alienist sent down to examine Whitehead's mental condition. I have every reason to believe that Mr. Redmond did this. At all events, very shortly after Mr. Redmond's visit a couple of experts came to Portland Prison and examined Whitehead and Gallagher, and in the course of some weeks after they and some others of the Irish prisoners were released.

INHUMAN TREATMENT

The prison officials tried to make out that Whitehead was feigning insanity all along. In fact, up to the time he and Gallagher were released the doctors maintained that both of them, as well as the others, were perfectly sane, and merely shamming insanity, and they kept on punishing these poor lunatics for shamming insanity. I have a copy of a prison report on Gallagher's case submitted to the Home Secretary by the prison's visitors. Such documents are painful reading, but the truth about English methods has got to be told, and so I will give their own official report, taken from their Blue Book, and let it speak for itself :—

" As to Gallagher's treatment, we find in September 1887 he, according to the report of the medical inspector and medical officer, commenced feigning insanity, and since that time he has been constantly under medical observation, and he has also incurred 16 punishments for refusing to go out to labour and using improper language to officers. In October 1888 he commenced vomiting his food, and continued to do so until February 1889, *and thus managed to reduce himself into a very low state.* He was admitted to the infirmary, and the vomiting ceased, and shortly afterwards—in March 1889—was discharged from the infirmary. . . . He was re-admitted in September 1889, and has continued under medical treatment till the

19

present time (*that is, 19th April,* 1890, *when the report was sent in*) for debility caused by persistent vomiting, which the medical officer believes to be voluntary, and pretended insanity. Dr. Blandford describes him as subdued and reticent in manner, with a downcast eye full of suspicion, and said that his manner appeared to indicate that he felt that he had been foiled in his attempt to deceive, but that he was still playing a part, and he thinks he is a dangerous man, who will require very careful watching and management."

This was the sort of reports the English Home Office wanted, and they got them, and meanwhile the torture of the insane prisoners went on.

When Dr. Gallagher was finally released Dr. Ferris, the New York specialist who examined him, pronounced his recovery hopeless, and attributed his insanity solely to the treatment he had received in prison. Dr. Ferris said in his report :—

" I see his companion, Whitehead, is also demented. The prison officials must have treated these men cruelly. Gallagher's condition is worse than death. The torture we are told he received during the first five years —now that we know he is insane for eight years—must have been very severe. The punishing of this man for shamming was cruel in the extreme. No one who sees Gallagher two or three times could for a moment doubt the reality of his insanity. To mistake his acts for shamming is inexplicable.

" (*Signed*),

" ARTHUR WARREN FERRIS.

" Savoy Hotel, New York City,
September 7th, 1896."

Dr. Gallagher is still living. He has been in a lunatic asylum on Long Island, New York, since his release in 1896. Whitehead, on his arrival in America, was also examined by experts, and likewise pronounced to be hopelessly insane and placed in an asylum. Such is the " humanity " of England's prison system where Irish political prisoners are concerned !

III

A SKIRMISH WITH INSPECTOR LITTLECHILD

IT must not be thought that Gallagher and Whitehead received any worse treatment than the other prisoners. By no means. Generally speaking, we were all treated alike, for the authorities deliberately set themselves to drive us all mad or to kill us, and they succeeded in doing this with most of our number. Some of us realised this situation early in our imprisonment, and saw that the mercilessly savage treatment was meant to smash us, and three of us, Daly, Egan and myself deliberately set ourselves to defeat the officials' design. It was a fight against frightful odds. On the one side were the prison authorities, with all the horrors of their prison machinery, relentlessly striving to accomplish their objects with unlimited ways and means at their disposal. On the other side were the prisoners, each standing alone and friendless, but resolved never to give in, with nothing to sustain him in the fight but his own courage and the pride he had in being an Irish Fenian, without encouragement save the sympathy and cheering words coming to him every now and then from his plucky and self-reliant comrades, fighting the same fight as himself, in the same spirit of " no surrender." Throughout the whole time we stood loyally by each other, and, as I have said, were in close and constant communication with each other. Never a week passed but I received a voluminous note from John Daly—and some weeks two or three notes—and he received the same from me. This went on for about eleven years. As with Daly, so with Egan, for the eight years he was with us. Tell that to the prison authorities and they would say it was utterly impossible. But we, too, had reduced our business to a scientific system—it was diamond cut diamond. At all events they never had the satisfaction of catching notes with either of us.

Several times I got terms of thirteen days' punishment for notes of mine being found with others of the prisoners.

With what pleasure I used to look forward to getting these bulletins from them and the nervous delight with which I would peruse them and the peculiar satisfaction I used to feel at our being able to outwit Harris and his satellites and enjoy such luxuries in spite of all their precautions and carefully laid traps.

Egan's notes would sometimes be illustrated with comic sketches, and they used to afford me many a chuckle and quiet laugh in the corner of my cell. At Christmas time we all wrote verses to each other—verses more

treasonable perhaps than poetic. I cannot
remember any of Daly's or Egan's verses,
but have by me a copy of one of my own
effusions, and a few verses of it will serve as
a sample of our prison rhymes and show the
spirit in which we were facing the Chatham
music.

My Jimmy, dear,
Another year
Has snail-like crept away
Since you I wrote
That " P. P." note,[1]
My gift last Christmas Day.

And I again
Unearth the pen
To try what I can do
At stringing rhyme
This Christmas time
For comrades staunch and true.

Another year
For Ireland, dear,
We've spent in these drear cells
Where England strives
To blast our lives
With torments fierce as hell's.

But their worst we scorn,
For we're Fenians born,

---

[1] On the previous Christmas I had written to Daly and
Egan a skit on Pontius Pilate, *alias* Governor Harris

A SKIRMISH

And, by heaven, the same we'll die ;
　No slaves are we,
　We bend the knee
To none but God on high.

　Ah ! no, old man,
　They never can
Our Fenian souls subdue,
　For our love is bound
　Too firmly round
Our cause to prove untrue.

　Here's to our land,
　May she withstand
The might of England vile ;
　May the future bring
　On swifter wing
True freedom to our Isle.

The " pen," to which I referred in the second verse, was the prison name we had for my tiny bit of blacklead pencil. This I used to conceal by burying it in the floor of my cell. Thanks to Daly we were rarely without a " pen "—he kept us supplied.

Not only had we to exercise the utmost care and craftiness in writing and transmitting our correspondence, but we had also to very carefully get rid of the notes after reading them. It would never do for one of them to be found—it would mean thirteen days' punishment for the writer, if not for others, besides making the officers, if possible, more vigilant than ever.

There were perforated iron ventilators built into the walls of our cells, and these masked horizontal air shafts. They formed very convenient waste paper receptacles, for anything pushed through the ventilators dropped down a foot or so into the air shaft and could not be seen. While the *Times*-Parnell Commission was on, and before we had yet been visited by Inspector Littlechild, of Scotland Yard, or had heard a word about the Commission (in fact, I may say that during those years we heard practically nothing from the outside world) one day returning from labour I was halted in the corridor on my way to my cell by the search warder and questioned as to how long I had occupied the cell I was in then and had I been putting paper into the ventilator. It was the duty of this officer to search our cells at uncertain times, and for this purpose he was armed with hooks and spikes and a bull's-eye lantern and other paraphernalia for examining the chinks and crevices and suspicious angles of the cells.

The search warder removed the ventilator of my cell and got a coal scuttle full of material that had once been paper. Away he went to Daly's and Egan's cells, and some other cells as well, and found about an equal quantity in each. In reply to all interrogations we protested our ignorance of how the material had got there.

The prison authorities knew that somehow

we were able to carry on a clandestine correspondence. This they were aware of from their having captured a few notes by accident. Finally they thought of the ventilator in the cells, and eager to find some scrap of evidence that could be used by the Government at the *Times*-Parnell inquiry they ordered the ventilators to be opened and searched. No doubt the private and confidential corrsepondence of John Daly and other Irish Felons in Chatham Prison would have a peculiar value if they could only get hold of it, and so ventilators were torn down and many buckets full of material taken out. It was carefully, very carefully examined, but all to no purpose, for not a single note was ever put into the ventilators without first being put into the mouth and reduced to pulp by rolling it between the hands. That is the history of the private and confidential correspondence of certain treason-felony prisoners in Chatham which the Government did *not* produce at the *Times*-Parnell Commission.

Shortly after this incident came Pigott's visit to Daly and Inspector Littlechild's interview with the so-called Irish-American prisoners with a view to getting informers to give evidence before the Commission.

Some ten or eleven of us were one day kept in our cells after dinner instead of being turned out with the others in the usual way for labour. As I waited in my cell that evening, wondering what this meant, I could hear one after another of the others in the cells before me taken away and then brought back again after intervals of half, or three quarters of an hour.

Presently came my turn, and I was marched away and ushered into a cosy little room, where I found Mr. Littlechild sitting at a table in front of the fire. He and I were old acquaintances. He was in charge of the party of Scotland Yard officers who arrested Dr. Gallagher and myself in London ; it was he who had charge of working up the case to convict us.

Soon as I got inside the door I was met with a bland smile and a " Good day, Mr. Wilson ; how are you ? " That was the first time I had ever been addressed as " Mr." in prison, and I duly made note of the courtesy and suspected he wanted to work something out of me. " Good day, Inspector ; what's up ? What has you here ? " With a considerable lot of hem-ing and ha-ing Littlechild started off spinning a rambling kind of a yarn about nothing in particular. Now, I knew that Mr. Littlechild did not come all the way to Chatham for the mere pleasure of telling me that kind of thing. I knew Scotland Yard methods, and that he was there to do a stroke of business, so I cut his rigmarole short with—" I say, Mr. Littlechild, never mind beating about the bush, just tell me what you want with me and I will give you an answer." " Oh, just so, Mr. Wilson ; thank you very much ; 'tis a pleasure to talk to a sensible man like you, etc. Well, you must know that there has been a Special Commission appointed by the Government to investigate certain allegations that have been made against the Irish Parliamentary Party. These allegations are to the effect that there is a connection between that party and the Irish Revolutionary Party in America, and that the workings of the one party are made to serve the purpose of the other. This question at the present time excites the greatest possible interest right through the country, but especially in Ireland. Most of the Irishmen prominent in public life are to appear and give evidence before the Commission. In fact, everyone is anxious to go forward as a witness. Certain persons in London, knowing that you came from America in connection with the skirmishing movement, believe that you were in a position there to enable you to speak authoritatively on the subject. These persons have sent me down here to see you so as to give you an opportunity of also going forward as a witness before this Commission to say what you would wish to say about the matter. There is no reason why you should not have a chance of appearing as a witness any more than the others, like William O'Brien or Michael Davitt, etc." "Now," said he, dipping his pen in the ink, "I am ready to take down anything you'd wish to say."

My answer was brief and to the point. " Look here, Mr. Inspector, if a single word of information would get me out of here to-morrow, sooner than give it to you I'd prefer to remain here till the day of judgment. Please take that as final."

I rose from the chair thinking that that had closed the interview, but it hadn't. Mr. Littlechild was not to be choked off so easily. He talked at me for about three-quarters of an hour, complimenting my intelligence one moment, calling me a damned unpractical fool the next, and so on. I said very little —in fact, scarcely anything—beyond reminding him at every turn when he paused for breath that " I was not the scoundrel he would like to have me, and that I had given my answer." He threatened, he appealed, and when his bullying did not work he tried gentleness. He was the stern police officer one moment and the sympathising kind friend the next. He would contrast my life in there as a prisoner with life outside as a free man. Why should a man like me be cooped up there with the blackguardism and ruffianism of the country and be subject to all the misery and degradation of convict life, denied God's free air and the love and sympathy of friends and everything else that goes to make life worth living ; neglected even by those who were really responsible for my being in prison, for after all I had been used by others. There were they enjoying the sunshine and pleasures of life—going about with plenty of money in their pockets and caring no more about me or my sufferings than if I were a disgrace to them. He gave me to understand that if I would only be " sensible " (as he phrased it) not only would it mean release for me but also a job in the Civil Service.

At length the hateful interview drew to a close. Littlechild snapped out, " That will do," and I got up and was making for the door and the escort that awaited me outside to see me safely back to my cell. As I was about leaving Littlechild said : " Well, now, look here, Wilson " (he had dropped the " Mr." early in the interview) " am I to understand and report to those who sent me here that you refuse to give me any information to prevent the commission of crime ? "

I replied : " Mr. Inspector, you are to understand that I refuse to give you information for any purpose whatever."

" Well," said he, " when you go back to your cell and think this thing over coolly, you will probably change your mind ; in fact, I know you will. If you do just drop me a line. The Governor will give you pen, ink and paper. Scotland Yard will find me. Good day."

I went out and the escort brought me " home " to my cell. The uppermost feeling in my mind was wrathful indignation at this outrage put upon me by the authorities.

When next due to write a letter I wrote to a friend telling of Littlechild's visit and what my answer was, and telling what I thought of the authorities for compelling me to receive such a visitor on such a business. That letter was suppressed, but I was allowed to write another in lieu. This second letter was written in practically the same terms. That also was suppressed, and again I was allowed fresh paper to write another. When the Governor notified me of the suppression of the second letter I asked him what was the reason for the suppression of these letters because the authorities did not wish me to inform my friends of Inspector Littlechild's visit and the offer he made me. After a short pause the Governor said : " No ; it is not." I then wrote the third letter, telling about the visit and my reply to Mr. Littlechild, but avoiding anything in the nature of blaming the authorities. That letter was despatched all right, and the friend to whom I sent it returned it to me after I was released from prison. It is now in my possession.

IV

IT was not the fault of the prison authorities if Littlechild's mission wasn't more successful. If making things hot for us could have prepared the way for his success, he certainly would have succeeded. We were never so mercilessly or savagely dealt with as we were for two or three years previously. In the preceding winter I underwent some forty days' punishment inside of three months. It had been an exceptionally cold winter, and, after taking from me portions of my clothing, I was put into the coldest cell in the prison —one that was known as the Arctic cell. Some time before I had to complain to the director about this cell being so frightfully cold that I had known the thermometer on frosty days, with a north-eastern blowing, to stand some degrees below freezing point. I got forty days' starvation and solitary confinement in that cell. Talk of hunger and cold ! Many a time I was forced to chew the rags I got to clean my tinware in an effort to allay the hunger pangs.

One day when I was nearing the end of this punishment, wanting to leave the cell for a moment, I put out my signal. After a while the officer came and let me out, and then stood looking over the corridor railing, apparently interested in the ward below. I went off along the corridor, and nearing the end my heart gave a great jump. There on the floor beside one of the cell doors were several pieces of broken bread. I was absolutely starving and could have eaten it ravenously, but like a flash a revulsion of feeling came, and in my impotent rage and misery I uttered curses fierce and bitter against English villainy as ever Irishman uttered. The blackguard officer, whose name was Membry, had got me thirteen days of the long spell of punishment I was doing, and, not satisfied, he had put that bread there thinking that in my famished state I could not resist taking it. He stood pretending to look into the ward below, but his eye was on my every movement, and had I touched the bread he would have pounced upon me and taken it from me, and would have had me up before Pontius Pilate to be awarded still more punishment for " stealing bread." Many will think such incidents incredible, and before I went to prison I should have thought them incredible too.

By the time I had finished that terrible forty days I was so weak and exhausted that I was unable to straighten myself or to stand upright, and I could not walk without staggering like a drunken man. Being absolutely exhausted I applied to the doctor to be put on light labour for a while, as I was unfit to do hard labour. It was customary for any prisoner who applied to be put on light labour, to have his request acceded to, because light labour entails a corresponding reduction of food. But my application was refused, and, exhausted as I was, I was kept at hard labour and had to work out my salvation as best I could.

Twenty-three of the forty days I had been sentenced to was given me by the Governor on a false charge. An officer charged me with having a piece of newspaper in my possession, though I knew no more of it than a person who had never stood inside the prison gates. However, some years afterwards, I had the satisfaction of honestly earning the twenty-three days with compound interest, for I managed by an underground channel to get in newspapers wholesale for about two years as well as to carry on communication with outside friends without being suspected. How this was done will be told in the next chapter.

It was at this time I read a copy of Mr. Gladstone's second Home Rule Bill in the *Weekly Freeman*. I got the paper while at labour, and the question was how to get the bulky thing into my cell, for only in the cell and on Saturday evening would it be possible for me to read it. The paper contained not only the bill but the debate on its introduction. My usual way of dealing with a newspaper was to tear out the most interesting paragraphs and articles and bring them into my cell one at a time concealed in my under-clothing, somewhere easy to come at in case of emergency. The uninteresting portions I destroyed at once. But I could not deal with the Home Rule Bill and debate in this way, for it filled several pages, and it was, need I say it, so very interesting that it would have to be brought into the cell entire and read, re-read, and studied.

To meet the rub-down search that was certain, and the special search that was possible, I got a piece of brown wrapping paper and tore it into the shape of an insole for my boot. Then folding the *Weekly Freeman*, I put it into the bottom of one of my boots with the paper insole over it. From this it will be seen how neat and well-fitting our boots must have been. My next move was to make a needle. The mere making was not a very difficult task, as I was a tinsmith, and had the tools necessary to do the job, but to do it and the rest without letting the officers suspect anything required rather artful dodging. But at this time dodging the officers' eyes and dodging the prison rules had been reduced to a fine art by Daly and myself.

Well, when the bell rang to knock off labour I was ready with the needle in my mouth so that I could quietly spit it out in case of emergency, and the newspaper in my boot prepared for either " rub-down " or

special search. There was no special search
that day, and of course I got through the
rub down easily enough, and as soon as I
got to my cell I ripped open my mattress
and placed the newspaper in the centre of it
under the cover and then threaded my needle
and sewed up the mattress again. Your old
convict has always some thread hidden away
somewhere in his cell.

All this occured sometime in the middle
of the week, and when Saturday afternoon
came the mattress was again ripped open
and the paper taken out and the remainder
of the evening was spent reading the
speeches, studying the Bill, and making
notes. Next day, Sunday, I passed the notes
to Daly with the paper and the needle so
that if he was not able to finish the reading
before turning out in the afternoon he could
do as I had done, conceal the contraband in
his mattress.

Talking of newspapers reminds me of the
first and only time I edited a paper. It was
in prison in the worst days of the Chatham
régime, while I was working as a stereotyper
in the printers' shop. Daly, in his notes to
me at this time, took to writing in newspaper
style, using the editorial "We" on all
occasions. Entering into his humour I told
him I would give him a head-line in a week
or so to show him how a thing of that kind
ought to be done. So I set myself the task
of printing a newspaper, or rather a sheet

resembling a newspaper, for news I had none. It certainly was a difficult thing to attempt under the eyes of the five officers in the shop, who had me, as an Irish prisoner, singled out for special surveillance, and it had to be carried through without arousing the slightest suspicion. As a start I made "pie" of a couple of formes I had got to stereotype—that is, I loosened the quoins or wedges and spilled the type all in a heap. Then I went to the officer in charge and reported this "accident," and asked him to allow me to take down some cases from the compositors' department to my own corner and re-set the job. I got permission, and brought down the cases and was ready to start on my newspaper. Of course, I wasn't going to waste much time sorting the "pie," and instead of going into the cases it went into my melting pot. I worked at my paper at every odd moment I could, and it was only occasionally I could get a few minutes unobserved, and after eight or nine days I got it up after sundry accidents and close shaves of being detected. The next difficulty was to get it printed, for each machine and press in the shop had men working round it, and I had to be just as careful of them as of the officers, for they would have been only too glad to give me away to curry favour. It was out of the question to approach any of them, but necessity is truly the mother of invention. "Any port in a storm," I thought, and turned to my stereotyper's oven. This I saw would answer the purpose. A stereotyper's oven is an apparatus closely resembling a letter-copying press, and I placed my first page on the bed of the oven, inked it, and laid the paper on the type, brought down the top plate, and applied the necessary pressure. It printed beautifully, and in turn each page of my newspaper was printed off. It was on tissue paper, because ordinary paper would have been too bulky to escape the everlasting searches.

Anyhow, on Sunday I delivered the paper to Daly, and his coughing and chuckling in his cell that evening told me how he was enjoying the perusal of it. I have said that it was a newspaper without news, but in appearance, except that it was printed on tissue paper, it might easily be taken for a newspaper just come in from the outside world. In capitals on the top of page one was the name " The Irish Felon," and under that in small capitals came the information—" Printed and Published at Her Majesty's Convict Prison, Chatham, by Henry Hammond Wilson, Saturday, such and such a date." The leading article was as treasonable as a leading article could well be. Next followed a page of what purported to be news, then an essay on prison philosophy, and I had one page illustrated. The illustrations were wood-cuts of convicts who had escaped from prison, and whose portraits had appeared in the *Hue and Cry*. A couple of the most villainous-looking of these pictures, with " criminal bumps " and all that, were made to stand for the infamous Sadlier and Keogh, and served as pegs upon which to hang the story of these renegades' base betrayal.

Another meek and harmless-looking photo was made to stand for that wise old gent who was supposed to be versed in all ancient lore, and who wrote interestingly upon the domestic policy of the Lacedaemonians—this old party, when interviewed by the representative of " The Irish Felon," had a great deal to say about England's Prison System— very little of it complimentary. Of course, there was a poet's corner where I dedicated some verse to Pontius Pilate *alias* Governor Harris, not very complimentary to that gentleman, commencing with :

The song I'll sing
In the air will ring,
  Of Pontius Pilate O !
That thundering thief,
Our Chatham chief,
  The grunting dog you know.

I forget the rest of it, but the last verse ended :—

So come along
And raise the song,
  Damn Pontius Pilate O !

THE CHATHAM " IRISH FELON "

Pontius Pilate little suspected that while he and his assistants were striving with might and main to destroy us, body and mind, we were indulging in such amusements and having such gibes at him.

V

AFTER working some time as a tinsmith in Portland Prison, where I had been engaged at making oil bottles, cannisters and various kinds of tinware, I was shifted out to the yard to the job of packing the manufactured articles.

When changed to this packing job I hadn't an idea where the tinware I had to pack was being sent to. I merely got orders day by day to pack certain classes of the goods into the cases supplied to me for that purpose. When I finished packing, the cases were immediately taken up to the prison store rooms out of the yard where I worked.

My curiosity was aroused almost as soon as I started on the job as to where the enormous quantity of tinware was being sent. Setting myself to discover this, I soon learnt that the prison authorities had a contract with the Admiralty for supplying such tinware as was used by the English war vessels, and that this tinware I was packing was sent up to Woolwich Arsenal.

This gave me an idea which I at once set myself to work out.

For the purpose of clearly understanding my narrative it will be necessary to explain that one side of the yard I worked in was occupied by the carpenters' shop. The tinsmiths' shop adjoined the carpenters' shop, and formed a second side to the yard, while a sawpit shed and entrance to the yard formed a third side, the fourth side being a blank wall.

Communicating with John Daly, who was then working in the carpenters' shop, I asked him to try and plane me up a thin piece of stuff, something like a Venetian blind lath, and to manage to drop it out of the shop window into the yard so that I could get it. John, of course, did as I requested, and I smuggled away the lath without the officers inside or the sentry who had charge of me outside noticing anything. I had some black paint for stencilling purposes in connection with lettering and numbering the packing cases, and I gave the lath a coat of this paint. After it was dry I got a piece of chalk (supplied to me for keeping count of the tins I packed) and wrote on the lath :— *" For God's sake throw in a piece of newspaper —any old newspaper— and earn the gratitude of a long term convict."* The packing cases were all numbered, and the one I then had ready was No. 24, and it was to be packed full of five-gallon oil bottles, and these were to be packed with cocoanut fibre. The handles of the bottles were all placed upwards, and I ran my lath with the chalk-written message through the handles of three

43

or four of the bottles in such a way that whoever unpacked the case could not fail to notice it. The packing finished, No. 24 was sent away, and in due time it was returned empty to the prison. It was nearly dinner-time the day it reached me in the yard, but I was so anxious to know whether it brought anything that I couldn't wait till after dinner, so I at once unscrewed the bolts, lifted the lid, and peeped in. The case appeared to be full of newspapers. I hastily closed the lid down again and re-fastened it. There was scarcely time to finish when the bell rang out to knock off labour.

After the usual routine, parading and searching, we of the Penal Cells lined up in our usual places ready to be marched off to our cells. While waiting, Daly (who, of course, knew all about the game I was on) and I got the opportunity to exchange a few words. He had noticed the arrival of No. 24 in the yard, and at once inquired— " Well, anything ? " " Yes, a donkey load." " Good Lord, what can you do with them ? " " Can't say yet ; will think it over in the cell."

In the cell during dinner hour I thought out a plan of dealing with the situation, which I proceeded to put into execution after our resuming labour.

On getting back to the packing yard I moved *the* case into a blind corner between the tinsmiths' and carpenters' shops, then got a couple of lids of other cases, and with these made a platform on each of the two front sides of the case. Upon these platforms I proceeded to pile up as many bottles as they would hold. All this was done with a view of making it difficult for any of the officers to get near the case when I removed the lid and got inside it.

Having secured all the approaches as far as possible I was then ready to take off the lid. It was hastily removed, and I jumped inside and lost no time in putting the newspapers out of sight by placing them all at the bottom and arranging the cocoanut fibre packing on the top. When satisfied that everything was right I wet the packing and then jumped out and went over to the sentry and told him, with an air of great concern, that the packing in that case was very wet, that if tinware was packed with that fibre there would be such damage to the bottles that they would be rejected and returned, and that someone would get into trouble. I suggested that he should allow me to take the packing out and spread it on the timbers in the sawpit shed, where it would dry out in a very short time. The sentry went over to the case and examined the packing ; finding it quite wet he adopted my suggestion, and ordered me to take the packing and spread it in the shed, and then he moved off—that very obliging sentry with his rifle at the shoulder, pacing backwards and forwards a few feet away from me, his chief business being to guard me and see to it that I was guilty of no infringement of prison rules or of any irregularity.

I at once set to work at securing the newspapers. I got into the case, caught up a small bundle of the papers and secured them inside my waistcoat, then gathered up a bundle of the wet packing, holding that in my arm so as to conceal the lump under my waistcoat, got out of the case and over to the shed, and from behind the timbers arranged the packing to dry, and at the same time concealed the papers ; then made another journey back and forwards, and kept on repeating this until I had all the papers in safety. Day by day for a long time after this I examined portions of the papers— that is, I would take some papers with me when going to the closet and look through them. On discovering a "newsy" bit I would, after reading it, tear it out and take it back with me to be put in concealment in order to be passed on to Daly later.

From this time onwards newspapers of various kinds kept coming into me in fairly good numbers, and what a heavenly break it was on the hideous monotony of convict prison life !

At length I decided to try and get into communication with friends outside through the medium of Woolwich Arsenal. It was not difficult for me to get a sheet of tissue paper, as the high-grade tin that was supplied to the prison came to the tinsmiths' shop packed with a sheet of tissue paper between the sheets of tin to protect the surface. I provided myself with a sheet of this paper and wrote three different notes on it. One was to the nameless friend in Woolwich Arsenal, who was sending me the newspapers. In this note to him I asked him to write his name and address on the sheet and then send the sheet on to London to a lady whose address I gave, stating that he would get in return a £5 note for himself and a bundle of newspaper cuttings. I told him the £5 note was for himself and the newspaper clippings would be for me, and to send them in the usual way.

The second note on the tissue paper, addressed to the lady friend in London, merely asked her to send on the sheet to my old colleague, Jim. She would understand what I meant, and sent on the notes to James F. Egan, who had been released from Portland some time previously.

The third note, addressed to Egan, read something like this—" Dear Jim, I got a taste of the gold fish you presented to Jerry; 'twas delicious. X also got a taste and pronounced it good. He is well, and has gone in for acrobatics over Wee's good luck. Please attend to request in above first note. Regards from X and from D1."

The note to Egan was written in a kind of Prisonese, the translation of which is as

47

follows :—" Dear Jim, I got a read of the newspaper you sent to Blank (a prison officer) ; it was very interesting. John Daly also got a read of it, and was delighted with the news. He is well and in the best of spirits. Attend to above (Woolwich Arsenal) business. Daly sends regards. Same from Henry H. Wilson."

The note to Egan, written in the way I wrote it, was a guarantee to him of its genuineness. He was certain when he received it that it came from me, for only Daly or myself could have written it, and only the three of us could understand the language of it—that language had been manufactured by ourselves for the purposes of our prison correspondence.

This note went through all right and reached Egan, who lost no time in attending to the business. He and Dr. Mark Ryan went down to Woolwich to the address given on the tissue paper note, and interviewed my nameless friend (he was an Englishman, now dead, otherwise this story would not be written now) ; they gave him the £5 note and a bundle of newspaper cuttings ; the latter came into me all right and were a delightful treat. Egan made the selection, and knew what was likely to be most interesting. This arrangement went on for some time, and I then got ambitious and devised a plan of escape from Portland Prison, which I was satisfied would be successful, if I could only have the assistance of a reliable confederate outside the walls to work in co-operation with me. The question of safely communicating the plan outside seemed to me the principal difficulty in connection with the matter. To overcome this difficulty I decided to communicate the plan in shorthand to Egan as being the less risky way of sending it. Egan and I could read each other's shorthand. Up to this no shorthand had been used in the notes passing through Woolwich Arsenal. My nameless friend never suspected I was anything else than an ordinary convict up to the time of Jim Egan and Dr. Ryan's visit to him. After that he knew he had been showing kindness to one of the Irish Political Prisoners, consequently I feared a note sent to him that would be all in shorthand might alarm him, so I determined before saying anything about the plan of escape to send a note through him to Egan in ordinary writing, but with a short paragraph in shorthand. This I thought would to some extent familiarise him with the shorthand, so that in the following one, which of necessity would have to be a bulky one, he would not baulk at the volume of shorthand. However, that second note was never written, for the reason that a few days after I dispatched the other with the shorthand paragraph an order came down to shift me from the tinsmiths' party and work I was at, to another party and other work.

49

VI

LEARNING A TRADE

IT is popularly supposed that prisoners are *taught* trades in English Convict Prisons. Such was not the case during my time in Penal Servitude. At most they may get opportunities to pick up one or more trades. That is, a prisoner might be put into one of the trade shops and be given some tools and some material and get a piece of work to do which in reality would be extremely simple to the ordinary tradesman in the shop. It would not be explained to him how he must set about doing the job, yet they have a class of officers known as " trades warders," who are supposed to understand tradesman's work, but these officers do not teach trades to the prisoners—as a matter of fact, they only visit the shops occasionally and then but to give orders concerning what jobs are to be done, never to *teach* a prisoner how to learn a trade.

The green hand in a shop may by observation pick up how to do his first piece of work—that is, by keeping an eye upon how the old hands do things. After a time, the new hand, should he master the simple work, gets other work a bit more difficult ; that finished, he gets something still more advanced, and so on step by step.

50

LEARNING A TRADE

If the prisoner lacks observation or has no
aptitude for the work, he may, as happens
with a great many prisoners, remain in the
shop for years, and at the end know very
little more about the trade than the first day
he was put to it. What I state in reference
to learning trades is accurate as far as it
applies to the ordinary convict. But in the
case of Irish Political Prisoners this business
of learning a trade was a frightful experience,
because of the countless opportunities it
afforded to the officers in the trade shop to
wreak vengeance upon us—opportunities that
were fully availed of. In this connection it
must be remembered that at the time of
our conviction all England was panic-stricken.
The English imagination got rattled and
started to work overtime at high pressure
speed. There was blood on the moon and
a skirmisher or Irish Fenian to be seen at
every turn.

The panic was at its height when we were
arrested in London. Immediately the howl
went up for vengeance. A special Bill
dealing with the situation was introduced in
Parliament by the Government of the day
and passed into law in record time. If I
remember rightly, that Bill was introduced,
read the necessary number of times in the
Commons and House of Lords, and received
the Royal signature, all in about twenty-four
hours. However, to come back to our conviction, once inside the walls of the Convict

Prison we were soon made to realise that the prison gates closed out from us a great many things that we had been familiar with in the outside world. But the prison gates did not close out from us the spirit of vengeance that was holding sway throughout England. That spirit held inside the walls with far greater intensity than it did outside ; it was the atmosphere of the place all the years we were there right up to the end. Now, to come back to the matter of learning trades. Let me take at random the trade of tinsmith and my own early experience in learning the trade.

The first day I was put into the shop the officer in charge gave me a set of tools—hammer, rasps, soldering irons and a quantity of soldering liquid—he showed me a place at one of the work benches and told me my place at work would be there at the bench beside a soldering stove. A number of partly completed oil bottles were placed on the bench before me and some bottle necks, and he told me to " go ahead and solder the necks to the bottles." Never having been inside a tinsmith's shop in my life before I hadn't the remotest idea how to set about doing the job, and I am sure looked as foolish and awkward as I felt. It was out of the question to ask any of the prisoners around me how I should do the soldering— to have done so would have brought me three days' bread and water punishment on

a charge of " speaking to another prisoner,"
nor dare I stand there doing nothing, that
would have brought me three days' bread
and water with the accompaniment of
" plank bed " on a charge of " idleness
during working hours."

Although new to the tinsmiths' shop I
was at this time quite an old hand at the
game of learning trades, as I had already
mastered several of them, so knowing the
ropes I started in to make things a bit lively
for myself by holding up my hand and going
to the officer and quietly informing him
(what, of course, he already knew) that I
knew nothing about tinsmith work, and was
at a loss to know how I was to do the
soldering. Then the expected happened.
That officer glared at me and roared at me,
and proceeded to empty the vials of his
wrath upon my wooden head for not knowing
how to do such a simple thing as solder a
seam ; I was the limit of stupidity, and, in
his opinion, there was so little brains in that
numbskull of mine that, by God, he wondered
whether I knew enough to eat my dinner
when I returned to my cell. I knew better
than to interrupt him ; were I to do so I
would get three days' punishment on a
charge of " Insolence to an officer." However, he exhausted his stock of nice talk on
me for the time being, and came to a stop
by sarcastically inquiring if by any chance I
could condescend to open my eyes and look

at the way the men beside me were soldering, and advised me to waste no more time idling but to get to my work and solder damned quick. The soldering seemed very simple, indeed, when one watches a workman doing it. Smear on some liquid on the tin, heat the iron, and apply the solder to the joint and make the seam with the heated iron. How many times by my mistakes have I given the officer a chance to open out and lash me with his tongue ! My iron not hot enough or my iron too hot, and the tinning burnt off it or trying to solder without cleaning the iron, or trying to do it, and forgetting to apply the " spirits," and so on, at each mistake I got it—his jeers, his scorn, his sarcasm, his outrageous insults. But, merciful God ! why need I go over it again —day in, day out, harassed and worried at each step. On it went from week's end to week's end for years, until the trade was mastered. No sooner had I arrived at the point of being as good a tradesman as any other man in the shop, and thus becoming, to some extent, free from continuous nig-nag, than I would be shifted off to another shop to make a fresh start to learn another trade, with the full accompaniment of incessant harassing, and then having, after years of learning, mastered that one, only to be again shifted off to learn another, and so on.

From the *cleaners' party* I was moved off to the foundry, where after four or five years

LEARNING A TRADE

I learnt *iron moulding*; out of that away to
learn *stereotyping*, then on to learn *japanning*
and *stencilling*, from that to *carpentering* and
joinery; mastering that shifted off to learn
tinsmithing; from the tinsmiths' shop to
learn *wood turning*; after mastering that set
at *pattern-making*—continuous performance for
almost sixteen years.

The officers of the prison—whether in
Chatham or Portland—left nothing undone to
make life miserable for us. During the day,
whether at work, on parade, or in our cells,
they harassed us all the time. During the
night it was the same, especially during the
years when they were applying the " no
sleep torture "—while this lasted we never
could get longer than an hour's sleep at a
time. Then it was the sterling friendship of
manly comrades counted for much. Then it
was, John Daly and James Francis Egan,
that I learned to know your nobleness of
soul. Yes, when your own hearts were
wrung with anguish under the torture you
were suffering, no weak cry, no coward's
whine fell from you. You were men all the
time, you had only a pleasant face and a
word of sympathy in your cheery notes for
your younger comrade.

VII

BOBBY BURNS OF CHATHAM

ONE of the most extraordinary characters I met whilst inside the prison walls was "Bobby Burns." He was certainly the strangest, and in a class all by himself. Bobby had been born in Ireland, but lived a long while in Scotland, where he had been convicted for forgery, I believe.

From the point of view of the prison authorities Bobby was one of the worst characters, if not the very worst, that ever came inside a convict prison gate. Yet Bobby Burns is associated in my memory only with kind thoughts—kinder thoughts than I have for any prison official—be he priest, parson, doctor, or warder.

The first time we became aware of Bobby's existence was on a certain Sunday in Chatham when we Irish political prisoners were at exercise, monotonously walking around the ring in the prison yard, with a ten-pace distance between each two, several officers being in charge of the party. All of a sudden we heard a terrible smashing of glass ; it came from one of the cell windows overlooking our yard ; the glass was being rapidly smashed, pane by pane, as if with a sledge-hammer. The whole thing only took a few seconds, but it was a clean job—not a particle of glass remained in the sash. Immediately could be seen the jolly smiling face of a prisoner clutching the iron guard-bars with both hands. His first words were —" Cheer up, boys. To hell with the Crown and Constitution. I wanted to see you as I heard you were Irish Fenians. God save Ireland. Maybe you'd like a song," and off he started to sing " Who Fears to Speak of Ninety-Eight ? " He had a loud voice, and that song seemed to ring all round the prison. Our officers had tried to frighten him down by shouting at him and shaking their clubs at him, but Bobby quite ignored them. All the same he didn't get far with the song ; the officers inside had interrupted him and pulled him down from the window, and the next thing we heard was the sounds of scuffling, jangling of key chains, and Bobby's howls of pain as the officers beat him with their clubs. Then we heard the cell doors close as the officers left his cell, and immediately Bobby was up at the window again to resume the song as if nothing had happened.

For many a Sunday after that Bobby appeared regularly at the window and sang Irish songs for us. I don't think there is an Irish rebel song known to me that I haven't heard Bobby sing during those Sunday concerts. Of course, all the time Bobby was liable to interruption by the officers coming in and pulling him down and beating him, but just as soon as they would go out and close the cell door Bobby would get up to the window again and continue as if nothing had happened. Sometimes he used to inform us in a kind of stage whisper— "That was Parker and Beel (or whoever it might be) in murdering me."

At times Bobby would vary the programme by introducing an impromptu speech full of "local colour." We heard him on a variety of topics, but his pet subject was "English Humanity as illustrated by the Convict System of the Country." Certainly Bobby should have been an authority on the subject. He had been through the whole course— flogging, penal chains, parti-coloured dress, dark cells, silent cells, penal cells, semi-dark cells, No. 1 scale and plank bed accompaniment, and all the other varieties of punishment for torturing the human mind and body.

Poor fellow! All the time we knew him he was constantly under punishment. Punishment, some of it sanctioned by prison rules, but the worst and more brutal punishment inflicted upon him at the whim of the individual officers. The officers had every opportunity to do this in the lonely separate cells. Many a time we have heard poor Bobby "done up" in his cell. At times he would get frantic and rave and howl like a frenzied lunatic. At times, when he would keep this up too long, he would be brought over and put into one of the " silent cells," below where we were located in the penal cell. He could there howl all he wished, but no word of it could be heard outside once the cell door closed upon him. These " silent cells " were dark, and with their peculiar cone-shaped roof were specially constructed to allow no sound to escape out.

The hand of every official in the prison was against Bobby, and Bobby's hand was against them. Yet he was not by any means a vicious character. As far as I could learn Bobby's bad conduct started over a question of religion. He was a Presbyterian, and on certain week days he, in common with those of other Protestant denominations, had to attend services in the Church of England Chapel. Bobby protested and refused to go ; and kept on refusing and getting punished for this every time. However that may have been, he certainly had no respect for prison rules, and at the time we knew him he appeared to treat with contempt all prison rules and regulations ; his voice was always to be heard, speech-making or singing, loud laughing or howling with pain from beating —Bobby couldn't be subdued.

On one occasion Bobby was awarded a flogging—thirty-six lashes with the " cat "— officers and everyone else thought that would subdue him for a while at least. They brought him out to the yard and fastened him up to the " triangle " (all floggings took place outside the cell windows of the Irish political prisoners) and gave him his flogging. He was then taken back to his cell, and the doctor had the usual large plaster of zinc ointment applied to his lacerated back. In a couple of hours after, when the officer opened the cell door to inspect him, he found Bobby sitting on his bed-board with one knee thrown over the other, his arms folded and his cell pot (the only thing allowed him in the punishment cell) jauntily placed on the side of his head for a hat, and Bobby himself singing at the top of his voice an old popular music-hall song—" Oh, we'll carry on the same old game."

Poor Bobby ! I believe he died in Chatham before we were shifted away.

Speaking of Bobby's treatment reminds me of another prisoner who worked for a while with me in the foundry. This was George Barton, who was decidedly feeble-minded, and afforded great amusement to the officers, and, indeed, to most of the prisoners, by his queer, uncouth ways. George worked the handle of the coal-grinding machine in the foundry. This was the only work it was safe to put George at, as he had merely to keep on turning the wheel.

One day a brute of an officer named " Bully Parker " came to the foundry door and stood speaking to the officer in charge. Parker caught sight of George in the corner beside him (I worked in the opposite corner) and went over and said something to George.

I didn't catch what it was, but I saw Parker draw back and give the poor simpleton a terrible kick in the stomach. George gave a wild yell and fell down unconscious. Parker dashed out laughing. The officer in charge bade one of the other prisoners bring over some water, and after a while George regained consciousness and was helped to his legs— he appeared to be in great pain—sobbing and crying he leaned on the wheel for support.

I went over to the officer in charge and made application to speak to the chief warder when he next came around, then went back to my work. Soon after Principal Warder Ruffel came in, and I was brought over to him, and I made complaint to him of what had happened, Barton all the time crying and moaning. Ruffel went out, and after a few moments two assistant warders came in and took Barton to the infirmary. I never saw him again, but I heard he died in a very short time after being taken to the infirmary.

I told of this incident in a letter soon after the occurrence ; that letter was suppressed, and should be found amongst the other suppressed letters, etc., in the Prison Department of the Home Office.

The English convict prisons, as I knew them, contained a motley assortment of criminals drawn from the different strata of English society. The ex-M.P. was there, the banker and ship broker represented ; we had lawyers and doctors, policemen and soldiers, artisans and labourers, wastrels and scoundrels of various degrees. As the years passed, on they came, criminals all, thousands of them, passing in from the gutters of English civilisation and passing out again. I had them for companions—these criminals, guilty of almost every crime in the calendar, ranging from the multi-murderer down to the courtmartialled soldier. But let that pass. England might force me to associate with the dregs raked in from the gutters, might shave my head like theirs, and stamp the Government broad arrow all over me ; humiliation might be heaped on to me with an unsparing hand, and punishments—diabolically brutal—measured out for years, but never for one moment did I forget I was an Irish Political Prisoner, and, in spite of it all, never felt any degradation. On the contrary, I wore that convict garb with a certain amount of pride, and took satisfaction in the thought that all her laws and with all her power this great England could not force me —one of the mere units of the Irish rank and file—to regard myself as one of the criminal class any more than I could ever be forced to regard myself as English.

The struggle for Irish freedom has gone on for centuries, and in the course of it a well-trodden path has been made that leads to the scaffold and to the prison. Many of our revered dead have trod that path, and it was these memories that inspired me with sufficient courage to walk part of the way along that path with an upright head.

VIII

THE GOLDEN RULE OF LIFE FOR A LONG SENTENCE PRISONER

IN the course of these articles I have referred at length to the brutal severity of the prison treatment of the Irish political prisoners, but in this connection, up to the present, I have only dealt with what might be termed the crude brutality of our jailers—such as the long spells of starvation punishment, the no sleep torture, the perpetual harassing, etc. But besides punishment. of this class there was another and more refined kind that seemed inspired by a spirit of devilry and aimed at galling the finer feelings of a man's nature and was calculated to blur and deaden the moral sense. As an instance of this class I will mention the " Special Search," which occurred frequently—about twice a month through all the years. On these occasions we would be stripped stark naked and subjected to the most minute examination of our person—so minute that oftentimes the bull's eye lamp was used. Had this search stopped short at a minute examination of the hands and between the fingers, of the soles of the feet and between the toes, of the mouth and inside the jaws and under the tongue, it would be disagreeable enough ; but it went further, and to such a disgustingly indecent extent that I must not here do more than imply the nature of it. This search would sometimes be carried out to the officers' accompaniment of a running fire of comments in keeping with the nature of the work they were engaged in.

Besides this search we were subject to the ordinary " rub down " search at least four times a day. In this the prisoner merely unbuttoned all his clothing without removing it, and the officer carefully felt him all over. I have been obliged to complain to the prison authorities of the indecent and hurtful way some of the officers mauled me while subjecting me to this search. That complaint will be found entered up in the official " Complaint Sheet " with my other records.

When the English Government, in 1848, decided to degrade the Irish political prisoner to the level of the ordinary criminal and passed the Treason Felony Act, they did not tell the world it would be part and parcel of the game to try and debase his mind and sap his self-respect. Nevertheless, such undoubtedly seemed to be the spirit and design of the authorities in their attitude towards the political prisoners during my time.

I have before me at the present moment the official document handed to me by the Governor of Pentonville Prison the morning I was released. It is a " *Licence to be at Large*," and is dated from " *Whitehall*, 21st

day of September, 1898," and goes on to
state that "*Her Majesty is graciously pleased
to grant to Henry Hammond Wilson, alias
Thomas James Clarke, who was convicted of
Treason Felony . . . her Royal Licence to be
at large. . . ." "This Licence is given subject
to the conditions endorsed upon the same. . . ."*
This is the endorsement referred to :—
"*This Licence will be forfeited if the holder
does not observe the following conditions.*"
Then follow four conditions, No. 3 of
which is as follows :—
"*He shall not habitually associate with
notoriously bad characters, such as reputed
thieves and prostitutes.*"
This document is signed, "*M. W. Ridley.*"
That is, by the Home Secretary of the day,
Sir Matthew White Ridley.

Lying before me is another document—a
letter written by myself in Portland Prison—
when I had been nearly fifteen years in
prison. The letter was addressed to my
brother and was sent out to him. He gave
it back to me after I was released. The
following extract from it will serve as a
standard to measure up Sir Matthew White
Ridley and his No. 3 condition and those
concerned :—

"I had a letter from Mrs. ——, and was
a good deal amused with her idea that the
life I was living in here was something like
that of a Carthusian saint or a 'Rapt
Culdee.' Bless the woman's soul ! That

would never do at all. When a mortal man feels in all its bitterness what it is to have the delicate curves and tender angles of his human nature rubbed up and currycombed against the grain, *then* is not the time to ' rub salt in ' from within by interior nig-nag and self-inflicted worry. Why, man alive, had I set to work on those lines, endeavouring to cultivate a lackadaisical tone of mind, my wits would have been gone years and years ago. No. *Clinch your teeth hard and never say die.*

" *Keep your thoughts off yourself all you can.*

" *No mooning or brown studies.*

" *Guard your self-respect (if you lost that you'd lose the backbone of your manhood).*

" *Keep your eyes wide open and don't bang your head against the wall.*

" These and a few others, which the deferential regard my prison pen has for *The Rules* prevent me from mentioning here, are ' *The Golden Rules of Life for a Long Sentence Prisoner,*' that might be found hung up in my cell had I any say in the furnishing of it."

In magazines, etc., one oftentimes comes across articles dealing with England's prison system. In these it will be noted that the keynote of the system is " humanity "— developing the better nature of the erring brother and all that.

I never found the slightest trace of any such spirit inside the walls ; on the contrary, when I let my memory go back to those times, and turn where it will either in Chatham or Portland, I can only find brutal persecution, and this spirit found its way into every little detail of the daily routine. For years we political prisoners were not allowed slates—all other prisoners were supplied.

For a long while I never got any but girls' and boys' trashy story books, when I was due for a library book. When I complained to the Governor about the matter, and asked to be given some kind of books that would be adapted to my educational rating, he ordered the escort to take me away, and next time I became due for a library book they gave me a volume of nursery rhymes—" Ba, Ba, Black Sheep, have you any Wool," " Little Bo Peep Fell Fast Asleep," etc.— infantile rhymes of that class and nothing else.

Some time later on, they gave me an extraordinary book. I forget the title of it, but it was one of the fiercest anti-Popery books I ever read, although I had read through some hot stuff of that kind up in Ulster, where I was raised.

The next time I became entitled to write enabled me to put my complaint on record. I told of the trashy books I had been getting, of my complaint to the Governor, of the nursery rhymes result, and the virulent anti-Popery book given me—a Catholic—that was specially marked for " Protestants only." My letter was, of course, suppressed.

IX

MANY and strange were the expedients re-
sorted to in order to give occupation to the
mind, and thus save ourselves from being
driven mad. It was ever present before me
that were I to " let go " of myself madness
was inevitable. It required, at times, all the
effort I was capable of making to enable me
to choke off despondency and wrench the
mind away from dwelling upon the miseries
of such a life.

Looking back to those times memory
shows me a picture of myself in that white-
washed cell of mine, sitting with slate and
pencil, devoting hours and hours to all sorts
of calculations. Not only have I counted
every brick in my cell and every bolt that
studded the ironclad doors, and every perfo-
ration in the iron ventilators in that cell, and
calculated the weight of the bricks used in
building it, and also worked out the number
of bricks used in building the entire prison
and figured out the total weight. Yes, many
an hour have I spent turning that prison
inside out and upside down, re-arranging the
bricks of it into a pyramid one time or
into a square, and so on, and calculating
dimensions ; then, again, placing the bricks

end to end with a view to finding out what distance they would extend ; that done, place them side by side to see how far they would stretch by that arrangement, and after that build them up one on top of another to find out how high they would reach. As a result of calculations I could at one time have told the total number of buttons on the clothing of the entire population of that prison or the number of " broad arrow " marks that was stamped on their clothing. I have taken clippings of my hair for several weeks from the weekly cuttings, and measured these samples with a micrometer (one of the tools I used when pattern-making) and calculated by these measurements that over six feet of hair had been cut off my head during thirteen years.

On one occasion I got a volume of *Cassell's Popular Educator*, issued to me as a library book. It was the volume where the short-hand lessons commence. I started in to study them, and after mastering the lessons in that volume applied and obtained the other volumes one after the other until I learnt all that was to be got in them about shorthand. Then, by way of practice, I set to work on the Bible. Starting at the beginning of the Old Testament, I worked my way right through the whole book to the end of the New Testament, stenographing every word of it from cover to cover. That finished, I started again and went over the

same ground a second time. By the time I
had finished all this I could write pretty fast,
and was curious to know what my speed was.
As I had no watch or clock in the cell to
measure a minute for me I was puzzled for
a while as to how the test could be made.
However, I eventually hit upon an idea that
enabled me to solve it.

Away up in the turret of the prison church
was a clock that struck the hours. We could
hear the striking in our cells. I utilised that
clock for my purpose in this way. Sitting
with pencil and slate one evening, when I
knew by the quietness of the prison that it was
nearing seven, I waited till the clock started
to strike, and simultaneously I started to
write something from memory at my best
speed and came to a stop when the clock
finished striking. Counting the number of
words I had been able to write I made a
note of it. Next night I was again ready
waiting for the clock, but this time with my
finger on the pulse of my wrist. When the
clock began striking I began counting the
pulse beats, and noted how many beats were
made while the clock was striking seven.
Assuming that my pulse was beating at the
rate of a normal healthy man (seventy beats
per minute) and that it made a certain
number of beats in a definite period of
time, and that I was able to write a certain
number of words in exactly the same period
of time, I was able, by the simple Rule of

PASSING THE TIME IN PRISON

Three, to calculate the number of words per minute I could write.

In the long winter evenings in the cells we used to do a good deal of telegraphing, and continue it after turning into bed at eight o'clock. Many and many a night have I lain awake for hours in the dark holding converse with comrades in the various cells on our corridor, for telegraphing could be carried on between two prisoners though four or five cells might intervene—that is, provided the fellow receiving the message pressed his ear against the wall, making, as it were, an air-tight connection. By this means the listening ear could hear the slightest tap on the wall. The slightest sound with the finger nail, that would be quite inaudible to the person making it, could be distinctly heard by the air-tight ear in any of the four or five cells on either side of whoever was sending the message.

John Daly for many months had a chum in his cell that helped him to while away many an hour. This was a spider he tamed and trained, and many an intereting bulletin came from John concerning the whims and antics of his pet. John placed a standing order with me during this time for supplying all the moths I could capture in my cell for his spider. Flies were very scarce in the cells. Scarcity of food, I suppose, accounts for this, but in the season there used to be a great many moths, hence John's order; but as he himself will, I hope, tell the story of his spider later on, I must only refer to it in a passing way. So, too, with the poisoning of John in Chatham with belladonna. I saw him inside half an hour after the dose had been administered to him. We were being brought out of our cells after dinner to go to labour. Looking at him I saw at once that he was very bad, his eyes bulging and his tongue protruding. To my whispered question, " What's the matter, John ? " he replied with great difficulty, " Belladonna ; they've poisoned me." That was all he could say. A few minutes later, after we had been distributed to our respective labour gangs, I saw John drop and being picked up and carried away. A Special Commission was afterwards appointed to investigate this poisoning, and also the treatment of the treason felony prisoners generally. The result was published in a Government Blue Book.

After Dr. Gallagher, Alf Whitehead, and some others had been driven mad by the prison treatment something happened that made me feel sure for a time that I, too, was going smash. The thought was horrifying. My turn had come—going mad like the others. The torture of that experience is just as fresh in my memory to-day as it was at that time. The recollection can never leave me.

This is what led up to it. One evening, sitting in the quietness of the cell, there commenced a loud buzzing in my ears. I slapped my ears again and again to try and get rid of it, but the buzzing was persistent, and nothing I could do would remove it or ease it. I tried everything I could think of, but all to no purpose. All night long it kept buzzing away, and with a queer sickening feeling the thought came to me that I was nearing the insanity mark. I reasoned the matter out with myself there in the dark, and came to the conclusion that the tension on the nerves had been so great that the breaking point had been reached—that the system was breaking down, and that this buzzing was the first indication that I had noticed. While in the cell the noise kept buzzing away, but once outside I couldn't hear it—I assumed the noise of the working parties in the labour yards drowned the other sound. For several days this kept up—the buzzing, torturing me in the cell, while outside in the yards it didn't bother me. One evening on being marched back from labour to my cell, glancing up to the roof of the penal cells in the distance I noticed that a fresh telegraph wire had been run from the military barrack on the adjoining hill into the prison, and this wire was fastened right over my cell, in fact insulated at the ventilator opening that led from the cell—I could have shouted with joy. That buzzing after all was not inside of me, but came down the ventilator shaft into my cell from this telegraph wire on the roof. The cell looked less gloomy that evening when I got home to it.

X

EXPERIENCE taught us that while in our cells we never could be certain when the officer's eye was looking in at us through the " Judas hole."   The shape and colouring of this inspection aperture, together with the glass on the spy hole, made it impossible to tell whether or not the officer's eye was at the hole.   While patrolling the corridors the officers wore fustian shoes and moved about so stealthily that no sound betrayed him to the prisoner inside.   This made it very difficult to write or read notes with safety. Not being able to rely on sight or hearing to safeguard ourselves from this danger, nature after a time came to the rescue and enabled us to cultivate the sense of smell to a degree that would astonish mortals living in the world of this twentieth century civilization.

In the Penal Cells Building the tiers of cells occupied one side, and these opened on to corridors ; a plain wall with windows formed the other side of the building. These windows, for purposes of ventilation, were always left open ; as a consequence a current of air, carrying an " institution " smell, swept around the corridors and was carried into the cells by means of a shaft, the opening of which was overhead in the doorway outside. A prison has a smell peculiar to institutions where crowds of humanity are herded together in a building. I have noticed similar smells in asylums, workhouses, etc. However, the smell of a convict prison has an unmistakable individuality. An officer might slip along to the cell door as noiselessly as he wished, but some *foreign* smell from him, such as hair-oil, tobacco, blacking from his accoutrements, beer, etc., would be wafted into the cell to give warning to the prisoner inside of danger —that an officer was hovering around outside, probably watching in. For years I trusted to my sense of smell to detect the silent sleuth outside my door who was on the alert to discover infringements of the Prison Rules. Many a time it gave me timely warning. Never did it fail me.

I have referred to the multitudinous notes that passed between my comrades and myself. We got our supply of black-lead pencils for years from John Daly. He worked in the carpenters' shop and was able to secure all we needed for our purpose ; but on one occasion a note of Egan's with a piece of black-lead pencil in it went astray and fell into the hands of the enemy. The Governor —Pontius Pilate—at once gave orders that Daly was not to be allowed any pencil at

his work—that a piece of chalk was to be
supplied to him instead, and friend John for
a long while had to do carpentry work as
best he could without a pencil. We were
then in sore straits for pencils to write notes
to each other. At this time I was working
as a moulder in the iron foundry, and I set
myself at work to make some black-lead
pencils. I had some black-lead of the kind
used for cleaning stoves and grates, and there
was any amount of fire clay and also blue
clay in the foundry. I got a piece of fire
clay and dissolved a lump of it in water,
and after allowing it to stand for a couple of
minutes poured off the water (which, of
course, held minute particles of clay in
suspension) into another vessel, which I left
to stand till next day, when all the particles
of clay had fallen to the bottom. Emptying
off the water I gathered up the clay. I did
exactly the same with the blue clay, and then
mixed together the black-lead, fire clay and
blue clay in such proportions as I thought
would turn out when properly baked a good
writing lead. I rolled the stuff out into long
thin cylinders and brought them up to the
drying room, where all cores for use in the
foundry were baked. The prisoner in charge
of this drying room (I'll call him here by a
fictitious name), Billy Jackson, was very
friendly to me as I had done him a few kind
turns, and he always stood ready to oblige
me at all times. I got Billy to carefully bake

the pencils for me, and on getting them back found they wrote beautifully. But they had one very bad defect—they would not resist moisture. For our purpose it was absolutely necessary they should possess this quality of resisting moisture, as our safest place to conceal the lead pencil if a sudden alarm came was to put it in the mouth. Assuming that, the defect in my articles was due to their not being sufficiently baked, I again took them to Billy Jackson and asked him to pile up his fires and give the pencils all the heat he possibly could. Billy did as I asked, but it was all to no purpose, the pencils still would melt in the mouth. I tried again and again, altering the proportion of the black-lead and clays each time, but I couldn't manage it—they could not resist the moisture. I finally came to the conclusion that the trouble lay in the direction of their not getting a sufficiency of heat, that they required something more intense than Billy's drying room could furnish. At this time I was engaged at making solid cylinder castings that weighed about a ton each. In getting one of the moulds ready I inserted the pencils about an inch down below the surface of the bottom. When the mould was ready the ton of molten metal was poured into it, and, of course, the pencils an inch below the surface were subject to a terrific heat— a heat so great that the sand of the mould would be still glowing red hot for several inches all around the casting when it would be uncovered next morning. Upon digging out my pencils and testing them I found they were still failures—they would still melt. The fault obviously lay in the ingredients, but, of course, I was restricted to the materials that were at my disposal.

Failing in this, it occurred to me that the crucibles used in brass foundry work were made of graphite, so I told Billy Jackson my troubles, and asked him to try and get me a few pieces of old crucible the first time one got broken at the brass foundry beside the drying room. It was not long till Billy had a few pieces for me, but on testing them on a sheet of paper I found they wouldn't do, as the molten brass had penetrated the graphite when the crucible was in use, and this grit tore the flimsy paper when I tried to write.

Again I told Billy my trouble, and explained that if I could only get a bit of new crucible I was certain it would make a good pencil. Billy struck a melodramatic attitude and asked, " Do you want a piece of new crucible ? " I said " Yes." " Then wait a second," and over he jigged to a dark corner singing

" The Marquis of Lorne
Had a little one born," etc.

He returned to the middle of the room

BILLY JACKSON

carrying a very large new crucible between his hands, again striking an attitude and in best tragedy tones he apostrophised the ceiling, " Romans, countrymen and lovers, Wilson wants new crucible and the gods are kind and are going to give him the wish of his heart." Crash went the crucible on the floor smashed to smithereens. I mildly remonstrated with him for doing this. He shook a reproachful finger at me as he reminded me it was only Government property. I took away a few pieces of the graphite. It served the purpose well, and the stock lasted until we struck luck again and were able to get real lead pencils.

Billy Jackson was an unique character. There in that dark, almost air-tight room, heated to nearly suffocation point, Billy was most of the time as merry as a lark—sometimes perched on the top of a big cask, with his arms folded, he sang his songs or his hymns with great gusto. He rarely got into trouble with the authorities, though. In fact, I only remember him to have been " reported " once. I was standing in the delinquent line that same evening waiting to be brought before the chief warder on some charge or other. Billy's turn came before mine, and when the officer preferred the charge against him—" whistling and making unnecessary noise in his cell "—the chief warder asked Billy what he had to say to the charge. Billy answered that he was only whistling in a whisper and didn't think he could be heard outside the cell. Chief Warder—" What were you whistling ? " Billy—" ' Jerusalem the Golden,' sir." Chief Warder to officer standing by—" Is that right ? " Officer—" No, sir ; he was whistling ' The Girl I Left Behind Me.' " " It won't do, Billy," said the chief warder, and Billy was sent on to the governor to get bread and water.

On one occasion I went up to the drying room to get some cores for the work I had in hand. Standing at the door, I signalled Billy. He told me to wait a bit, that he was busy. He was engaged at doing something at one of his fires. After waiting a few minutes, fearing the officer would get on to me for delaying, I shouted in to Billy to hurry up. He snappishly told me he couldn't as he was busy. He certainly seemed very intent upon whatever work he was doing. Finding the officer's eye off me I stepped in to the fire and found Billy with a piece of stick stirring something in an old swab can.

To my surprise I saw that the contents of the can seemed to be a rich-looking soup, with vegetables and other things in it. Inquiring what the deuce he was up to, Billy told me he was making turtle soup. " Wait a few minutes," said he, " and it will be ready and I'll give you some. 'Tis grand, I have made it several times before." " But," said I, " where in thunder did you get the stuff ? " Striking one of his characteristic attitudes he made answer in this fashion— " J464, there are more things in heaven or a prison hell than are dreamt of in your philosophy. Let me tell you I cleaned out my swab can, that's the saucepan, and I got water at the tap. When last over emptying ashes in the dust-pit, beside the cook-house, I sneaked some old cabbage leaves that were lying there. The screw's (officer's) eye was off me and I slipped them under my coat and brought them back. I got some Russian tallow from Hansford (the Instructor) —I have to get some for my work—but this was grand fresh stuff. I brought the bread crusts from the cell in my boots. It makes fine soup ; it is nearly done ; I'll give you some." Hungry as I was that concoction was too much for me, and I declined Billy's hospitality, but none the less I appreciated the generosity of that starving wretch's offer.

The last time I had a talk with Billy he asked me if I knew how poteen was made in Ireland (Billy was a Cockney). I described the process as well as I could, and then asked him why he wanted to know. He told me he had been reading an article in one of the magazines dealing with the making of poteen and that he intended to make some. I inquired how he proposed to do it. He said he had just got in two empty molasses barrels from the stores to break up for firewood. but that he could get nearly a quart of molasses out of them ; that, of course, he had any amount of gas pipe for core iron purposes that he could utilise for a worm, and that he had running water at the tap in the corner. A few days later I was moved off to another party, and never heard whether or not Billy succeeded in making his Irish poteen.

XI

A MEDLEY

WHEN telling of Billy Jackson smashing the big crucible, in order to provide me with a piece of graphite, and in an off-hand way closuring my remonstrance by telling me it was "only Government property," it reminded me of another occasion when I discovered I, too, was nothing more than "Government property."

It was out on the corridor of the penal cells one day when a number of prisoners had been paired off to cut each other's hair at the regular weekly hair-cutting. A crazy character, who imagined himself at times to be an astronomer, was paired with me. I knew my mad matey very well, with his head away up in the air, and his tense-drawn face, with the fixed, lack-luster eyes that told its own tale of insanity. I sat myself down on the stool, and off over my head at considerable speed capered his scissors, making the hair fly. It wasn't long till he "struck a snag" by giving my ear a nasty cut and causing some blood to flow. I tried to bring him down from the stars to mother earth by quietly remonstrating. Immediately the officer at the other end of the line bawled out, "Wilson, you are talking," and down he stalked beside me, and in a lofty, judicial tone, asked, " What are you talking to that prisoner for when you know the rules ? " I told him I was merely remonstrating against having my ear cut off, showing him at the same time my bleeding ear. " Oh, that's all very well," said he, " but you know the rules." " Yes," said I, " but am I to sit quietly here and allow my ear to be taken off ? " He quoted the rule—" Under no circumstances must prisoners be allowed to speak to each other," and told me if he found me at it again he'd " run me in " for bread and water. Then addressing himself to my mate, who had continued the clipping as if nothing had happened—" Look here, you will have to be more careful ; if I find you cutting that prisoner again I'll run you in also for damaging Government property."

I have bitter memories of this hair-cutting process in the early years of our imprisonment. These were the years when scissors were used. Fancy about a couple of dozen pairs of scissors in use to barberize about fifteen hundred men, these scissors at work every week-day were blunted and most of them with the rivets loose ; a pair of scissors of that kind in the hands of a clumsy operator made it terrible torture for the victim who was being trimmed. It was a sight when sitting in the body of the church on Sunday morning to look along the lines of cropped heads and see the havoc that had been

wrought upon most of the unfortunate lags'
skulls—regular ridges of cuts in many cases,
where the skin had been clipped away. In
later years the scissors have been discarded
and the hair clippers substituted, much to
the satisfaction of every prisoner who has
experienced the scissors clip.

Almost all the officers employed in the
English Convict Prison were ex-Army or ex-
Navy men. These were of varying grades
and classes—governor, deputy governor, chief
warders, principal warders, warders, and
assistant warders, civil guards, parsons and
priests, doctors and hospital nurses. The
great bulk of these were Englishmen and
Welshmen with a sprinkling of Scottish and
Irish. During my imprisonment I came in
contact with many hundreds of these officers,
and out of the whole lot I only experienced
unmistakable sympathy and kindness from
two. One of these was an Irishman and the
other was English—a Cockney. The Irishman
was a nurse in the Infirmary who, whenever
he had the chance, would throw in an extra
piece of bread into one of the Irish political
prison cells, and whenever possible would
whisper some interesting item of the news of
the day. I experienced kindness of both
kinds from him several times. It was kindly
for him to have sympathy. I knew his
two brothers well—both fine types of Irish
nationalists, but our prison friend had been
the wild boy of the family and ran away

when young and joined the English navy.
At the time we were experiencing his kindness
he was a navy pensioner.

The other—the English officer—was in
contact with me for several years, and I
received kindness often at his hands. When
the coast would be clear at work he would
sometimes nod for me to come over to him
—maybe it would be to tell me some news
from the outside world—something about
Ireland—sometimes to warn me to beware of
this prisoner or that prisoner, and not let
them see me doing anything, as they were
of the type to " give me away." One day
he gave me a great surprise. I was engaged
at my work and he called my name. When
I answered he ordered me to bring over my
rule. I took over the two-foot rule with me
and reached it to him. He took it, and in
the course of the talk that. followed he kept
shaking the rule at me as if he were taking
me to task for something I had done. He
first asked me if I knew anyone mixed up
in public affairs in Ireland named Pigott.
I asked was it Richard Pigott. He said yes,
and I told him I knew him as editor of a
paper in Dublin. " That's the fellow," said
he ; " he is a scoundrel, and is coming down
to see Daly one of these days." He reached
me back the rule, and in the rough, official
tone he roared out, " Go back to your work
and don't let me see you doing it again."
This, of course, was said for the benefit of

the other officer, who was stationed at the far end of the shop, as well as for the prisoners, to prevent suspicion.

Next morning I managed to get behind John Daly when we were being turned out for chapel and whispered the warning I had got. Pigott came that same day to the prison and visited Daly. I had a very long note from John on the following Sunday telling me all about his interview with Dick Pigott, but that story, as well as John's interview with Mr. Soames (representing the London *Times*) will not be touched upon here, as John will likely deal with them when he comes to writing his " Recollections of Life in Chatham Convict Prison."

It was not until years after, when we had been drafted from Chatham to Portland Prison, that I discovered, what had always been puzzling me, why the English officer singled me, the only Irish political prisoner in his shop, out from the forty other prisoners he had charge of to show me sympathy and kindness. He was married to an Irish wife.

The visits of Pigott and Soames to Daly were prior to that of Inspector Littlechild to us in Chatham which I dealt with in an earlier article. Judging by Littlechild's efforts it seemed to be very important for the purposes of the authorities that an informer should be secured in order to go before the *Times*-Parnell Commission with some story that would be damaging to the Irish side. But from what I know of the circumstances connected with the various English agents who were sent into the prison with the bribes, I feel certain that the authorities would rather have got hold of John Daly for their purpose than the whole lot of the rest of us. He was the important person. He was known far and wide among Irish Nationalists (Imperial Nationalists were unknown in these days) for his sacrifices and work in the National struggle, looked up to with admiration by the younger generation, and respected by all. The others of us of the younger school were mere rank and file workers, unknown, except to a very limited circle. For the purposes of those who were engineering the " trial " before the Commission any of the rest of us would not have amounted to much compared with John Daly appearing. However, I am certain that any one of the lot could have easily made terms for himself and secured release at the price of appearing. But those men—most of them under a life sentence—spurned the offer, and preferred to remain behind the bars for the remainder of their days, for at this time none of us had much hope of ever leaving prison alive.

I know the English sneer—it is often made use of, indeed, by people calling themselves Irish—" Put an Irishman on a spit and you'll find another Irishman to turn it," implying that the Irishman, on the patriotic side, is more treacherous and with less of a sense of honour than are men of other countries. Besides knowing a fair share of the history of Ireland's struggle for nationhood, especially in the last two generations, I have had the privilege of an intimate acquaintance with many of the leading spirits of the Fenian movement, such as James Stephens, Chief Organiser; John Devoy, Military Organiser, and the man who planned the Catalpa rescue, and took the military Fenian prisoners away from Australia out of the hands of the English Government; Col. R. O'S. Burke, who planned and successfully effected the Manchester rescue in 1867. The testimony of every one of them was directly to the contrary. Time after time the English Government offered huge rewards for the capture of well-known Fenians, and though in some cases there were thousands of Irishmen who *could* have betrayed them there were none who *would*. The whole thing is an English lie, started and kept up to discourage young Irishmen from organising to win the freedom of their country.

XII

THE SILENCE TORTURE

FROM time to time in the course of these articles I have had occasion to refer to that terrible " silent system " which prevailed in the English convict prisons ; these references were more or less casual.

A further word of detailed explanation concerning this system and its effects upon the prisoner, where the imprisonment is for a long term of years, may prove interesting.

The system, as it was applied in Chatham and Portland Prisons, might be said to depend upon the rigid enforcement of one of the prison rules, which read—" Under no circumstances must prisoners be allowed to speak to each other," to which should have been added, " or converse with anyone else," and we would then have the essence of the silent system. For be it remembered that not only must the prisoner hold no intercourse with his fellow-convicts, but it would be a punishable offence to attempt to talk to any of the prison warders, the discipline being such that the prisoner attempting to engage a warder in conversation would be almost certain to be hailed up under report and punished. As a matter of fact, should the warder fail to report the prisoner for such a violation of prison discipline, and one

of the numerous supervising officials come to
know of it, that warder himself would be
reported and punished. So strictly enforced
is this rule in its application to the attitude
of the prisoner to the warder that before a
prisoner can speak to an officer, even about
the ordinary work at which he would be
employed, he must hold up his hand to first
get permission to open his mouth. Should
he feel ill and wish to make application to
see a doctor he must hold up his hand and
get permission to make the report. Should
he want to go to the closet, again his hand
has to go up to get permission to ask, and,
of course, permission to go ; and so on all
through the day—the mouth, as it were,
locked all the time and only opened by
official permission.

Then, as far as the warder's attitude
towards the prisoner is concerned, he must
speak to him in terms of command, never
in conversational style. For instance, if I
were in my cell and required to be brought
before the Governor for any purpose, the
officer, after unlocking my gate and cell door,
wouldn't notify me in any such fashion as
" Come along, Wilson, the Governor wants
to see you." No. Instead he would bawl
out, " Wilson, attention ! " " Quick march."
Then as soon as I'd get outside the door he
would order, " Right turn " or " Left turn,"
as the occasion required, and off I would
march until such time as the Governor's

room door was reached. He would then give the order to " Mark time," and I would have to keep at that until the door was opened and the word given to " Forward." Into the room I'd go marching, and when far enough would be stopped by the command, " Halt." When the Governor would have finished with me they would bring me back after the same manner, marching and counter-marching, marking time and all the rest of it, with as much fuss and noise of military command as if I were a whole regiment of soldiers.

My purpose in dealing with the silent system now is to show that no matter who the man may be—educated or illiterate—no matter how hopeful his disposition or physically fit he be—no matter what strength of will power he may possess or what determination of character may be his to " see things through " in man's fashion, it will avail him nothing—he will inevitably be driven insane if only kept long enough under that silent system. It will gradually wear him down and shatter his nervous system and destroy the normal tranquillity of his mind to such an extent that a point will be reached when the mind becomes thoroughly exhausted and left in a state of frenzied unsettlement, having nothing to feed upon except such gloomy thoughts as will be dictated to him by his wretched environment. The end—insanity—for that poor mortal is then near at hand.

THE SILENCE TORTURE

That end comes sooner for some than for others, temperament being an important factor ; but speaking generally—all things else being equal—an educated man will be better able to hold out against the system than an illiterate man. In other words, the person who goes into prison with a mind well stocked with healthy ideas will take longer to break down than the person ill-educated, or who carries in with him comparatively few ideas. While the man with a well-stored mind stands a better chance when "up against" the silent system, yet no matter how well he may be equipped in this respect the system will win against him in the end.

In the early years of the imprisonment he may be safe enough whilst his memory furnishes him with subject after subject to give the mind pleasurable occupation as he turns them over. In this way thoughts and ideas one after the other are turned over and examined until finally the whole stock has been under review. Commencing again, idea after idea is examined afresh, but with far less interest than the first time; if no new view-point can be found when dealing with a particular idea. On and on this goes until the end of the stock is reached again. Starting again, it is found that some of the ideas and memories have no further interest ; the mind is sick of them ; they have been turned over so much that they are too stale to arouse any further interest. Such as remain and still retain interest are once more reviewed and turned over. Finally there comes a time when by this process of elimination there remains not a single idea of the original stock that has not been quite " played out " and has now become hateful. The silent system then wins, for the mind, though more or less enfeebled by this time, must occupy itself with something, and the dreary wretchedness and misery of the convict prison that have been kept at arm's length during the struggle now get their innings, while the spectre of insanity hovers close by waiting to take charge and complete the work of the silent system.

What I have described may be considered the negative factors that go towards producing insanity. The positive factors are the incessant harassing, the starvation punishment, and other punishments.

When tracing the effects of the silent system I took no notice of the library books supplied to prisoners. They certainly counted for something in giving occupation to the mind, and a good book counted for much in this direction. But the good book was a rarity, while many of the books supplied to me were a downright irritation—trashy books of fiction, stories of servant girls in love, stories of adventure for boys, stories for babies of the " Ba, Ba, Black Sheep, have you any wool ? " kind, and so on, were the class of books they generally threw into our cells. Very few of them contained anything

to supply healthy ideas that would be calculated to give occupation to a jaded mind.
It has been told in the course of these
articles how some of the Irish political
prisoners, recognising that the specially
devised brutal treatment of us, together with
this silent system, must either kill us off or
lead to insanity, decided, after comparing
notes with each other, to set ourselves at
work to devise ways and means of counter-
acting the effects of such treatment and thus
try and save our reason. Still, in spite of
all these efforts on our part, as far as I am
personally concerned, the increasing tension
on my nerves for some time previous to my
release was such that I felt certain, and still
feel certain, that another couple of years of
such treatment and I, too, like so many of
my fellow-prisoners, would have been driven
mad. But it was not to be. Instead, here
I am, with prison life a mere memory many
years old, jotting down some fragments of
the history of that experience. As I write
the season reminds me of many Christmas
times spent in prison and out of prison with
loyal old comrades. James Egan and John
Daly—they are in my thoughts. Egan has
gone from us, and lies in Glasnevin. Sturdy
Jim—loyal to Ireland and ever true to his
principles. And Daly—our own Daly—
maybe we'll spend this Christmas as we
spent last, and as we clasp hands pledge
" Our land alone and friends who owe
allegiance to her alone."

XIII

MINOR MEMORIES

IN jotting down these recollections I have taken hold of the facts at random, without any attempt to line them up in order of time. In commencing the story my intention was to select such incidents of prison experience as would be likely to interest readers of *Irish Freedom*, especially those of the younger generation. Proceeding to carry out this idea I was surprised to find that when dealing with some of the more vivid memories of those times there was brought back to my mind a number of minor memories that had lain sleeping for many a day—some of them, indeed, had been forgotten for years. I remark on this here as it has a bearing upon some of the incidents that will follow.

A day or two after having been sentenced the Governor, Chief Warder, and several other officers came to my cell in Milbank Prison. The Governor, as spokesman, explained the separation of convicts into two classes—one the Habitual Criminal Class, and the other composed of prisoners who had never been convicted previously.

In explaining the composition of the Habitual Criminal Class, he described them as a bad lot—bad in almost every respect—

and not at all the class of individuals that I would wish to associate with for the remainder of my life. I know now his description of that class was not far out. I had previously informed him that I had never been convicted before. He referred to this, and told me it was necessary that the authorities should get a guarantee from two reputable citizens vouching for me in this respect before they could place me amongst the first offenders in the " Star Class." He inquired would I give him the names and addresses of two such citizens. I had no objection, and gave him the names and address of two of my friends in America. He wouldn't take them—said it was necessary to have the names of persons resident in England, Ireland, or Scotland. Did I have any friends on this side who could answer for me ? I told him I had, but would not give him any such names. " That being the case," he said, " you will be classed as an Habitual Criminal and associate with convicts of that grade." I told him I did not like the prospect of that, and could not see why an assurance from people of standing in America, who had known me all my life, should not satisfy all requirements necessary to prevent my being obliged to associate only with the Habitual Criminal Class, more particularly because of the reasons I had for refusing to give the names of any of my friends on this side. As a matter of fact, there was in the back of my mind a strong suspicion that the whole thing centred round the question of the authorities trying to find out what connection there might be between America and Ireland, as far as our case was concerned, with a view of locating our friends in Ireland. It must be remembered that I was convicted under an assumed name, and up to the time of my conviction, and for long after, the authorities knew absolutely nothing about me—nothing beyond the fact that I had turned up in London and had been in Birmingham after having left a first trace in Liverpool. So I told the Governor I would give him no names on this side to assist the authorities to connect me with any person here. I would not be a party to having my friends persecuted by the attention of Scotland Yard. That, in the excited state the Government and English people were in owing to the arrest and trial of the Irish skirmishers it was absolutely certain that anyone known to be a friend of mine would be in for a disagreeable time of it because of the attention he would receive from the Government detectives. The interview ended by his giving me to understand there was nothing for it but to place me in the Habitual Criminal Class. Some time elapsed, and I found all my colleagues had been put in the First Offenders Class and were wearing the badge of that class—the Red Star—while I was isolated and wearing the ordinary convict dress. After a time, however, the Star was given to me and I was placed in the First Offenders division, and that, although no friend or acquaintance of mine had vouched for me.

Failing to get any information from me about my friends in "England, Ireland, or Scotland," on the friendly (?) pretence of not having me sent to associate with the Habitual Criminals, another attempt was made later on to ascertain my friends. The Governor had me brought before him, and a list of things that were taken from me by the authorities after my arrest was read out to me. The Governor explained that being a convict I had no rights and could hold no property of any kind, the authorities would send this property (money, watch and chain, etc.), to any friend I wished, and he wanted to know who he was to send it to. I gave him the name and address of a friend of mine in New York—John J. Morrison, an old Dublin man, who had been an Orangeman early in life, but who on getting away to America—away from his former environment—became a splendid type of active Irish Nationalist—as reliable and sincere as one would wish to meet. He is now dead, but John Morrison's name is still held in esteem by those of his old Nationalist colleagues who are still alive. The Governor informed me he could not send property to America, but would send it to anyone I would name in England or

Ireland. I refused to give any such name and was taken back to my cell.

On another occasion later on the Governor had me before him again and asked me had I any sisters. I told him I had. He asked their names ; I refused to tell him. He wished to know why I refused, and I declined to give him any reasons. " Well," said he, " an application to visit you has been received from Maria J. Wilson, of New York, who says she is a sister." I told him that was all right, she was a sister of mine, and I wished to see her. A few days later the Governor sent for me again to ask me would he turn over my watch and chain and other trinkets to my sister when she visited the prison. I told him by all means to do so, and also to let her have that money of mine which the authorities held. He said he couldn't do that, as the money had been turned into the British Exchequer and was now irrecoverable. When my sister came to the prison the authorities gave her everything that had belonged to me except the money, and the matter rested at that for years when, on my release, it cropped up again, but that will be dealt with later on.

In the long interval that elapsed between badgering me to get on the track of local friends, and the time when I was released —a matter of may years—time dragged along slowly through an atmosphere clouded with misery—weeks dragged along into months,

year piled on year, and meanwhile the
Treason Felony Prisoners had been dying off
one by one, or had been released after most
of them had been driven insane. In the
early years there had been over twenty of us
in Chatham Prison, and I was one of the
first of them convicted. In the latter days
there were only two of us in Portland, Henry
Burton and myself. He was ill and had
been taken into the infirmary, and I was
then the sole occupant of the Treason Felony
section of the Penal Cells—I was then up
against the dreariest spell of the entire
imprisonment.

It was then "strict silence" to the very
letter—all the more keenly felt because of
the contrast between then and the previous
years, when staunch comrades were giving
aid and comfort to me. John Daly had been
released months before, and James Egan had
been gone for some years. But the usual
routine of prison life went on in the same
monotonous fashion; the warders unlocking
gate and door and roaring out words of
command in the usual aggressive fashion;
the escort marching me off and reporting to
each superior officer he passed what his
"party" consisted of. "One man, sir,"
until he turned me over to other warders to
be searched and put to work, and after work
to be searched again, after which to be
turned over to other warders to be marched
back to my cells for meals or for bed, and

all this carried on without a detail of prison ceremonial omitted. As the time went on, month after month of it, I felt that my imprisonment was something like the sailor's rope that had no end to it.

Of the three comrades who stood in the dock with me and received the same sentence, Dr. Gallagher and Whitehead had been released years before, hopelessly insane, while Curtin had been released long before them suffering from a ruptured vesicle of the heart. Even yet I can't quite understand why the " reserved service " in my case. But this I do know, that no word or act of mine during that imprisonment has ever caused me any regret. I was then what I had been, and what I am still, an Irish Nationalist. I asked no favours, I got none, and I am proud of it.

During that dreary spell in the Penal Cells, when I was " bird alone " in the Treason Felony section, there was one other prisoner kept there permanently in the same building whose case caused quite a sensation when he was convicted. His name was Lee, and he was " Cleaner " in the Cells Building. Lee had been sentenced to death, but after the failure of several attempts to hang him he was reprieved and sentenced to penal servitude for life. The warders used to bring me out to clip Lee's hair, and he had to clip mine. On one of these occasions, while the warders were engaged together doing something or other, and with their eyes off us,

Lee got an opportunity to tell me the story of these several attempts to hang him. He described the escort on the morning of the execution, coming into the death cell with the chaplain, the pinioning of his arms behind his back, the arranging of the bag-like covering over his head, and the procession starting out from the cell to the scaffold, the chaplain all the while reciting aloud some prayers (the burial service, I think, he said). He graphically told of the frenzied feeling of fear that took possession of him as he got up on the platform of the scaffold and was placed standing upon the trap whilst the warders and executioner tied his legs and adjusted the rope around his neck. From the time he got on the scaffold he appeared to be dazed, and an awful stillness seemed to surround him ; the sounds around him as he stood there with his head covered seemed to be at a distance, but through it all the beating of his heart seemed to thunder in his ears. In fact, it seemed as if his heart had moved up to his ears. This was the state he was in when he heard a muffled voice in the distance say " Ready," and almost simultaneously he heard with terrible distinctness a bolt pulled back. He became collected immediately, and expecting the trap to give way—it didn't—after a second or two he heard someone say, " My God," and then could hear some whispering around him. Then he heard someone near him banging at the trap as if to drive it down ; some others got around the trap and tried all together to send it down by stamping on it, but all to no purpose, the trap wouldn't move. His legs were then untied, and he was taken back to the death cell and the hood removed from his head. He sat there for some time and could hear the hammering that was going on at the scaffold as they were putting things right. At length the escort came for him again, and off they started exactly as on the previous occasion—slow march, chaplain reciting the prayers on to the scaffold, legs tied, noose adjusted around his neck. On this occasion he seemed to take it all as a matter of course up to the point when he heard the word " Ready " given and the bolt snapped. His heart seemed to stand still, but again the trap refused to go down. He heard them dancing on it again, and they got a hammer and banged on it. No good. Off they took him again to the death cell. The chaplain intervened and begged the Governor to postpone any further attempts until the facts were communicated to the Home Secretary. The Governor consented, with the result that the Home Secretary reprieved Lee and sent him to penal servitude for life. He was released from Portland several years ago.

Printed in Great Britain
by Amazon